HOW TO BE HAPPY
(and great)
AT TEACHING
ELEMENTARY
SCHOOL

*Survival Skills you Didn't
Learn in College*

*There is no duty we so much underrate as the
duty of being happy. By being happy we sow
anonymous benefits upon the world.*
—ROBERT LOUIS STEVENSON

SANDY WILBURN PETERSEN, PH.D.

Printed in the United States of America

First Printing, 2020

ISBN: 978-0-578-82067-5

Book design by TeaBerryCreative.com

To Katie, who was born to teach.

CONTENTS

INTRODUCTION

Most new teachers *are* happy. They're happy to have earned their teaching credentials and happy that they've landed a job. They're excited about meeting their students and being part of a faculty. They're certain that they'll change the lives of children and make profound contributions to their school community. So why do nearly 50 percent of them leave the profession within their first five years of teaching?

Well, reality is a killer. Novice teachers discover they are not perfect teachers, parent encounters are unnerving, co-workers can be jaded, students are not angelic, and their workload is exhausting.

Every new teacher needs a crash course in mastering the daunting realities that can become impediments to success. It's easy to become disillusioned and join the ranks of bitter, critical teachers. If you want to love your profession, however, you'll need to step up to the plate and quickly master the practicalities of teaching that you didn't learn in your college studies: getting organized, bonding with parents, dealing with negative team members, feeling comfortable with your principal, building relationships with the kids, and all the other issues that matter every bit as much as pedagogy.

If you're looking for a book that bemoans today's unmotivated kids, poor parenting, unfair accountability systems, clueless administrators, pointless professional development, or anything else teachers love to complain about, put this book back on the shelf *immediately.* You'll hate it.

This book is about finding joy and success in your work. It is an acknowledgment of how blessed we are to be teachers and how we can move through our days in ways that fulfill us and allow us to be our very best for the sake of the children whose lives we touch.

IN THE INTEREST OF SELF-DISCLOSURE

I've taught almost every grade from first through college. I love teaching. I love (most) kids. I love (most) parents. I love (most of) my colleagues, administrators included. I also love a good, stiff drink, but that's another story. In the interest of full disclosure, you need to know that I have spent a good portion of my career working as an administrator. I have been a principal, a curriculum director, a staff development director, college professor, and an assistant superintendent in a large school district. Teaching, however, is my passion.

I consider it a deep privilege, and (most days) I can't wait to get to school. In my long and varied career, I have found no job as challenging, frustrating, and downright exhausting as teaching elementary school. Nothing even comes close. But there is also no job that can bring so much joy.

So, other than that stiff drink, what accounts for my happiness? That's what I want to talk about with you. As I come to the end of a very long teaching career, I want to share a few ideas and simple secrets to help you love your work, feel happy and fulfilled in your classroom, and transform that classroom into a joyful and productive place for yourself and every one of your students.

CHAPTER 1

CHOOSING HAPPINESS

The purpose of our lives is to be happy.
—DALAI LAMA

My mom loved a good feud. Nothing made her as happy as peeking through the kitchen curtains to critique a neighbor's choice of hairstyle, attire, parenting techniques, or anything else that offended her finely tuned sensibilities. She would sometimes burst out the door to share her opinions with the perpetrator. Mom wasn't afraid to confront a sales clerk, taxi driver, clergyman, relative, or neighbor who offended her. And offenses were frequent and often inexplicable. She once quit speaking to the woman next door who suggested that Mom's recipe for meatball soup could be improved with a quarter teaspoon of celery salt.

I must admit that I, too, have little fear of conflict, have an unyielding opinion on most everything, and enjoy a juicy tidbit of gossip. While all these predilections give me momentary satisfaction, they don't go very far in making me a better teacher or a better person, for that matter. And they certainly aren't qualities that make me happy.

On the other hand, I'm a hard worker, I'm reasonably well organized, and I enjoy picking out the perfect gift for family members and friends. Those are great qualities, if I do say so myself. I mention my own qualities, good and bad, for a reason.

THAT NAGGING INTERNAL CRITIC

Have you noticed the little voice in your head frequently tells you the ways in which you don't measure up? (I'm not the only one with a little voice, right? Yikes!) My little voice regularly compares me to others in a very unfavorable light. My little voice nags and points out all the things I'm not good at, haven't completed, or should have done but didn't. It's like walking around with a perpetual, and very opinionated, internal critic who just doesn't like me very much.

We certainly need to do an honest assessment of our own characteristics and determine which ones make us better and, perhaps, which ones might need a little remedial work. But, thanks in part to that internal voice, we too frequently focus on our negative characteristics without spending time celebrating all the good things about ourselves. Recognizing and acknowledging our positive qualities helps us maintain a level of happiness that isn't possible when we constantly focus on what we see as imperfections.

So, how do you see yourself? Is your glass half full or half empty? Do you usually choose to focus on what's right about yourself or what's wrong? How would you describe your basic disposition and personality characteristics? By shining a spotlight on our positive qualities, we not only find more satisfaction, we have a strong basis upon which to grow and develop into the person we were meant to be.

Reflection: What are some of my best qualities? What qualities help make me a good teacher?

NATURE VS. NURTURE

A favorite question in education and psychology is: Are a person's qualities the result of nature or nurture? My reply (and I told you I was opinionated) is: Who cares? Doesn't matter. If you care about nature vs. nurture, as far as happiness goes, there is an increasing body of research to demonstrate that we are born with our dispositions. Some people have a propensity to be happier than others because it's written in their DNA. Anyone who has had a child knows that some babies enter the world as happy and peaceful souls, while others are cranky and dissatisfied from birth. Some of us are naturally "glass half-full" kind of folks. Others, not so much. Again, doesn't matter. Our biological inheritance need not be our forever destiny. We can retrain our brains to look for the good, to find satisfaction in small successes, and to be optimistic despite our challenges.

So, say good-bye to the YES-BUTS:

- Yes-but...That's just the way I was raised.
- Yes-but...This is the worst class I've ever had.
- Yes-but... My spouse doesn't understand me.
- Yes-but...Our principal stinks!
- Yes-but...Half my class isn't on grade level.

An acceptable excuse for wallowing in misery is clinical depression, which can't be wished away or upended with a good dose of positivity. If you suspect clinical depression, get a diagnosis and accept treatment. Like everyone else, you deserve to feel good and be your best self.

Okay, there's another exception to the "For heaven's sake, pull yourself up and out of your misery and be happy" formula. Terrible things befall most of us at some point or other in our lifetimes. One of my daughters has a rare and life-threatening form of cancer. She and I and the others who love her aren't going to be singing "Polly-Wolly-Doodle-All The- Day" no matter how much of the old college try we give it. But there may not be a more critical time to at least try to look at the glass as half full as when we are faced with horrendous trials and challenges. I offer suggestions to help and support you, not to induce guilt or suggest that you must be ecstatically joyful every minute of every day. Some of us are experiencing pain because of those terrible and sometimes unexpected disasters that knock the wind out of our sails.

MEET YOUR OWN NEEDS FIRST

To be a positive and happy person, no matter our natural inclinations or the challenges we are facing, we must meet our own needs first. I can almost see some of you recoil at the apparent selfishness of that concept. I know, I know. As teachers we are caregivers. We are selfless humans who care little about salary, buy classroom supplies from our own meager incomes, and routinely work ourselves into a state of exhaustion for the sake of our students. Oh, please. Let go of that martyr thing, will you? Martyrs were burned at the stake or had their fingernails pulled out.

Always putting others first can lead to feelings of victimhood. We can feel underappreciated and, eventually, bitter. Who wants a bitter teacher? If you really can't put yourself first, at least put yourself in the same category as your students and others you care about. Treat yourself with the same thoughtfulness and respect you afford your family, friends, coworkers, and students. Get yourself in the mix. Nobody loves a martyr, and teachers seem to have a collective inferiority complex that leads to martyrdom. It's a nasty and unproductive point of view.

Teachers are professional people who have worked hard to attain a unique body of expert knowledge, and we typically continue to learn and grow throughout our careers. We need to be proud of our profession and ourselves. We need to be able to back up our strategies with research and best practices and be willing to articulate the hows and whys of our approach to the work we do. How can we expect the public to treat us with respect if we mope around bemoaning our status in the world and deferring to parents and legislators whose sole experience in education has been sitting in a classroom as students decades ago? Stand up and be counted as a professional and an expert...and earn that status by continually growing through reading, attending education conferences, observing colleagues at work, and other professional development opportunities. Never devalue yourself or your work.

SELF-CARE

None of this can be accomplished, however, if you aren't taking care of yourself. Like a car that's run out of gas, you just can't operate at peak performance when you are exhausted or overwhelmed.

If you are not taking care of yourself, it's very difficult to care for others. So let's look at your self-care habits for a moment.

Reflection: What makes me happy? What do I do for myself? How do I maintain my energy and positivity?

Those are the self-care questions I frequently ask teachers, and I'm no longer surprised by the answers I hear. They are almost always the same, divisible into two categories.

CATEGORY ONE: I don't have time to do anything for myself. This is most often followed by a sorrowful list of all the responsibilities they have and the people who are pulling them in various directions.

I sometimes push the issue by asking questions like "Could you just have sandwiches one day a week instead of cooking a complete dinner? Could you listen to some relaxing music on the way home? Could you give up one of your extracurricular activities at school?" The answer, from this group of harried and overworked individuals is always the same. "NO. I couldn't possibly do that. My husband, children, principal, etc. depend on me." Instead of feeling sorry for these frenzied souls, as I probably should, I find myself wondering why they think they are so important and irreplaceable. It seems to me that this is one more manifestation of martyrdom. No one is irreplaceable. Not me. Not you. Not them.

Heaven knows there are actual victims in this world. These are not the people I'm referring to. I'm talking about self-proclaimed victims who, on some level, enjoy playing that role. These are the folks who complain endlessly about how overworked and underappreciated they are yet take no steps to correct the situation. They mistakenly believe that others admire them or see them as noble and selfless, and that's a big perceived payoff for being a victim. If you don't want people walking all over you, don't lie down.

CATEGORY TWO: folks present a sharp contrast. Many of these teachers are pulled in just as many directions, but say things like this:

"I make it a point to..." This is followed by a seemingly mundane activity that the person does for herself to cultivate happiness:

- Never take work home on the weekend.
- Take a walk every day.
- Read a novel a month.
- Watch a Hallmark movie and eat Ben and Jerry's chocolate chip ice cream.
- Meditate.
- Keep a gratitude list.

Notice that almost nothing happy people mention costs a lot of money, except for the Ben and Jerry's, but there are cheaper brands. Some of those store brands are yummy.

> *Reflection: What am I doing for myself for relaxation and stress relief? What other things could I add to help me relax and refuel?*

Self-care is a good step to support your mental health. Too many of us think that taking care of others is important but taking care of ourselves is optional. That's just wrong, and it's a fast track to burnout.

YOUR BASIC NEEDS

Every human being (and teachers are human beings, no matter what our students may think) has basic needs. Remember Maslow? Assuming you are well-fed and have a roof over your head, let's simplify those remaining needs to the ones that most affect our outlook on the world and our success as teachers. In this chapter, we'll look at health and safety needs. Later, we'll talk about community, satisfaction, and self-actualization. How do these basic needs play out in our work lives?

YOUR HEALTH

When you don't feel well you can't possibly be at your best, so do all you can to take good care of yourself. Get regular health checkups and dental visits. If you've been prescribed medication, take it, and take it as directed. A good healthcare provider who knows you personally is a great investment. Dr. Google is full of errors and frightening predictions. Stay away from self-diagnosis.

What are you currently doing to maintain the best state of health you can have? I am frequently shocked at the amount of junk food consumed in faculty rooms. Sugar makes many of us happy, but it's a temporary fix that ends in a crash. Can you find healthy foods and snacks that you enjoy? I tried packing celery and carrots for a while, but I don't really consider that a snack, and so I felt deprived. After some trial and error, I discovered that, while I can't get terribly excited about nuts, if I mix them with raisins, the combination tastes delicious and satisfies my need for a mid-morning or afternoon pick-me-up. Yogurt is something else I enjoy, as well as a cheese stick or a hardboiled egg. These are grab-and-go snacks that can be tossed into your lunch bag in the morning. Or grab a week's worth on Monday morning, and you don't have to think about snacks again that week. I can hear some of you saying "Yuk." I'm not suggesting they should be *your* snacks of choice, but I am suggesting that you do some exploring until you find some things you truly like that are both nutritious and don't leave you feeling like a victim. Dip your banana in chocolate, if you must, but eat more banana than chocolate while you move toward healthy choices.

What about sleep? Bringing lots of work home is something that can keep you from the rest you need. Try to have a work cutoff time and stick to it. The smartest and happiest teachers I know bring home very little work and only as absolutely necessary. You can avoid the teacher homework habit by roaming the room while kids are working and checking their work along the way. The other benefit of this habit is that you don't have little Leroy making the same math mistake over and over through an entire page of problems. Nip it in the bud. Don't wait to discover his confusion until you lug those math papers home to check at the end of the day.

Rethinking your assignments to make certain that they are valuable and worth the time it will take you to correct them is also a good habit. By building in formative assessments as you teach, you can usually assess each child's level of understanding and sometimes determine that a written assignment isn't necessary. Of course, children need individual practice on some things, but certainly not on everything. Be judicious. Work smarter.

Your family, your spouse, your significant other, or your dog, cat, or parakeet deserve some quality time with you in the evenings. Stop lugging home a stack of work. Enjoy your evenings and go to bed at a reasonable time to wake up feeling refreshed, happy, and ready to tackle the day.

Reflection: Have I been neglecting any aspect of my health? What can I do to be as healthy as possible?

SAFETY

One of the biggest challenges to moving into the positivity zone is our natural bias to look for threats and danger. We are biologically programmed to keep a watchful eye out for the lion or the hostile tribe. Perhaps you've not seen a lion lately (though your principal may bear an uncanny resemblance to one) nor a hostile tribe for that matter (unless you've taught sixth grade), but you have seen an administrator charge into your room for an observation, you've seen an angry parent or a defiant student, and you've certainly seen your evaluations. We are met with challenges all the time, and we nearly always see them as threats to our well-being because, let's face it, they *are* threats to our well-being.

Realistically speaking, however, most (not all) of these situations are as much opportunity as they are threat. Some of the most affirming experiences of my work life have started as adrenaline pumping threats.

As the principal of an elementary school in an economically depressed area, I encountered frustrated and angry parents regularly. I NEVER welcomed that experience, and there were many of them. Let me share a few, along with lessons learned. Keep in mind, I DO NOT make this stuff up.

One mentally unstable woman stormed into my office, screaming, ranting, and frightening everyone in her path. Her eight-year-old daughter had gone home and claimed there had been a knife-wielding "slasher" in the cafeteria who had ripped her child's skirt with his eight-inch-long butcher knife. The principal, that's me, according to the story, had done nothing to stop the rampage. I tried in vain to calm the woman and assure her no such horrific experience had occurred. (Lesson #1 Do not argue with a deranged person. It serves to further incite them.) As it turned out, the frightened little girl had fallen and torn her skirt at recess time and, rather than accept culpability, had made up a creative, alternative explanation for the ruined skirt.

Eventually a restraining order had to be served on the mom because of her frequent, irrational storms of the school and our concerns for the well-being of staff and students. Her visits and public rants were unpredictable and frightening. So what good could possibly come from that?

The faculty, staff, and I learned a valuable lesson about possible situations our children might be facing at home. We learned to invite reluctant parents to the school and provide support and resources to help them cope with financial and emotional situations with which they were dealing. The parent connection had not been foremost in our minds to that point in time. Yet, as I dealt with more and more angry parents, I learned that they were frequently misinformed about what the teacher had actually said or done. The parents were often stretched to their limits emotionally so that a child's story of mistreatment could send them over the edge. I began to welcome (albeit reluctantly) the visits from angry parents by reframing them as opportunities to help and support rather than solely as threats.

As a result of what we were seeing, the faculty and I wrote

a grant to connect our school to local agencies that could provide medical, dental, and counseling services. We bought a washer and dryer for the school, began to offer nutritious breakfasts, and collected coats, boots, and other necessities that many of our parents were struggling to afford. Teachers brought in clothing their own children had outgrown, and we kept a storeroom of nice clothes. Because of the grant, we were able to provide after-school care where children were read to, tutored, helped with homework, played games, and given opportunities to learn both academic and social skills.

We invited parents to come in and see what their children were doing. Before long, we had moms and dads reading to groups of children, passing out cartons of milk and snacks, and speaking to some of the teachers, who always took the time to say hello and treat these folks with the dignity they deserved. We let them know about services we could connect them to and sometimes shared our own stories of struggling to raise our own children without all the resources we needed. (By the way, our teachers, because of the grant, were paid for these after-school activities, and teachers who chose, for whatever reason, not to be a part of the activities were never made to feel that they were less valuable because of that.)

Some of these parents, met with kindness and understanding, talked about difficulties they were facing. I met many single moms and some single dads struggling to make ends meet and care for their children at the same time. Often, they were angry and defensive. Visiting informally with the principal, teachers, custodians, and others who knew and loved their son or daughter, created a partnership for them.

The school became a refuge and support where the parent was neither judged nor ignored.

Ah, my "yes-but" friends, (who really should have put this book back on the shelf as I advised in the introduction) are now full of righteous indignation. I've heard it many times. "It's not MY job to feed kids or support parents. My job is to teach!" I get it. I hear you. I felt that way too once upon a time, until I realized that hungry kids can't learn, kids without coats or boots stay home during winter storms, parents who are at their wits end sometimes take out their frustrations on their children. We all need to feel safe and be safe to be our best. Teachers, children, AND parents. Maslow would tell you that's pretty basic.

A SAFE PLACE FOR TEACHERS

What makes us feel unsafe in our school environment? A group of professional educators working together can almost always create a safe environment. Leadership is required. Students need to know what the expectations are throughout the school and they must be the same from one classroom to the next. Respectful behavior must be expected and required. A support team of professionals trained to deal with severe misbehaviors and psychological difficulties needs to be in place. And last, but not least, administrators must support the teachers in every way possible.

> *Reflection: Are there places or situations at my school where I do not feel physically or emotionally safe? Why? What can I do about it?*

You will never be happy if you do not feel safe. You don't grin and bear it. Go to someone in a position to help. Be proactive, not just for your students, but for yourself.

HAPPINESS PRACTICES

Suzanne Degges-White in a *Psychology Today* blog (March, 2016) suggests four practices that can support your quest for happiness. They are friendliness, cheerfulness, compassion, and gratitude. I quite like them because they seem custom made for teachers. Wouldn't it be wonderful if you worked with a faculty who consistently displayed all those qualities? Oh, well. We'd better just start with ourselves.

FRIENDLINESS

We are made to be social creatures. Even the most reserved among us requires some human contact. And six hours a day with 6 year olds doesn't count. We all need friends, and we definitely need friends in our workplaces. Some very lucky teachers enjoy coming to work, not only to teach their students, but to spend time with their colleagues. I worked, once upon a time, in a school where teachers sincerely cared about one another. Lunch time was wonderful because we would catch up on one another's stories, laugh about the morning's frustrations, and offer support when and where it might be needed. We shared problems, suggestions, stories, and sometimes sandwiches, because one of the first-grade teachers often gave her lunch to a student who habitually forgot his.

The old saying "If you want to have a friend, be a friend" remains as true as ever. Smile, speak to ALL of your colleagues, even the grumpy ones. Help where you can. Not everyone will reciprocate immediately. For some folks, it takes a bit of time to warm up, but don't let that stop you. Be friendly not only to your colleagues, but to administrators, secretaries, cafeteria workers, custodians, parents, kids, and anyone and everyone you see. A smile and a warm greeting are always welcome.

CHEERFULNESS

Closely related to friendliness is cheerfulness. (Okay, I know this is starting to sound a bit like the Girl Scout motto, but what a wonderful world it would be if everyone strove to be cheerful.) Yup, you've got problems. Me too. We can walk around saying "Woe is me" or we can buck up. No sense in ruining everyone else's day. Besides, it is difficult to act cheerful without actually starting to feel a bit (or a lot) better.

COMPASSION

Everyone needs to be accepted despite their flaws. None of us are always at the top of our game. We fail and we fall short of being the person we'd like to be. Be loving and compassionate anyway to others and to yourself. It's so easy to pounce on flaws and to gossip and criticize. How about we cut one another a little slack! To be compassionate is far more difficult but creates an environment of caring where we all get to be human and make mistakes.

For some reason, it always seems more difficult to be compassionate with ourselves. When we miss the mark somehow, a less than stellar lesson, a child we just can't seem to motivate, a mediocre evaluation from our princi-pal, we can so easily label these setbacks as failures. Carol S. Dweck, in *Mindset* (2008), describes people with what she calls a growth mindset. These folks, always trying to improve, typically view their setbacks not as failures but as helpful information.

Right now I'm working on one of my lifelong goals. Learning to speak Spanish has topped my list of New Year's resolutions for more years than I would like to recall. Yet I've never really taken the time or made the effort to dig in and begin. Finally, this January I found an online program that began at the beginning and built Spanish language acquisition in what felt to me like a very sensible and linear process. Because the program was visual and auditory, I would not only read words and sentences, but hear them spoken by native speakers. There was plenty of repetition built in and the gradual acquisition of new vocabulary and grammar with lots of practice seemed custom made for me and my learning style. For a while I made great progress. Then things began to get more difficult. I had to ask myself if I was a failure or if my mistakes were providing me with valuable feedback on what I still needed to know and hadn't yet mastered. I realized, at one point, that I was learning as much from my mistakes as I was from any other aspect of my learning process. Making mistakes pointed out areas that needed to be reviewed and learned.

Not only did I redefine failure for myself, I also began to see success in a different light. I was not going to wake up one morning suddenly speaking flawless Spanish. That couldn't be my definition of success. Success had become a daily process of simply doing my best. In learning a new language or becoming a great teacher, isn't that enough? Never giving up. Learning from our mistakes. Starting anew every day. Moving in the right direction.

GRATITUDE

You can find a reason to be grateful every day of your life. You woke up this morning. Yay. You have a job. Yay. You get a paycheck. (Yes, I know, but yay anyway. It's better than nothing.) Many of us have health, friends, family, a dog who loves us, twenty-five kids who need us. We contribute to the world with our work. We have much to be grateful for if only we take the time to think about how lucky we really are.

These four practices, friendliness, cheerfulness, compassion, and gratitude, as conscious goals each day, will soon become our habits of life, helping us on our journey to becoming the teachers and humans we strive to be. The important understanding is that a person's level of happiness is not determined by external factors. You have the power to be happy within you.

Professionals in human resources are spending a lot of time these days talking about "soft" skills. I think these four qualities fall into that category. You were hired for your professional expertise, but employees also want to know that you are someone who will add a level of positivity to the school. No one wants to hire a person who will be cold, uncaring, or self-centered.

We all want to be around folks who are friendly, cheerful,

compassionate, and grateful for what they have. Those are qualities that can be cultivated. Mother Teresa famously said, "Be the change you want to see in the world."

> *Reflection: How do I currently live each of the happiness practices? What specific goal could I set to improve in one of the happiness practices?*

INTERNAL VS. EXTERNAL LOCUS OF CONTROL

Remember Rotter's Locus of Control Theory from your college days? In essence, he theorizes that some of us attribute our successes and failures to ourselves. These are the folks who have an internal locus of control with a strong sense that they basically have control over their own lives. Others, those with an external locus of control, tend to believe that they are the victims of circumstance.

Here's an example. You fail a test. Those with an internal locus of control are likely to say something like, "Well, I should have studied harder or paid more attention in class or not waited until the last minute and simply crammed for the test." Those with an external locus of control might say, "That teacher is so unfair" or "If he were a better teacher I probably would have done better on the test" or "That test didn't cover what it should have. No wonder I didn't pass." In other words, people with an internal locus take responsibility for both the good and bad that happens in their lives. External locus folks blame circumstances beyond their control.

What does this have to do with happiness? Well, victimhood is always a recipe for pessimism and unhappiness. The more likely you are to feel that you can control your world, the more likely you are to create an environment of your choosing...one that brings you happiness.

A neighbor of mine recently welcomed a new baby into the family, and I stopped by for a visit. In the course of our conversation she said, "Well, he looks like a nice kid, but we'll have to wait and see." I was flabbergasted. Wait and see? You're his mother! Don't you have some control over the kind of person this baby will become? What a perfect, albeit extreme, example of a person with an external locus of control.

There was also the woman who complained about what an unfriendly neighborhood we lived in. It really was a wonderful neighborhood, but because she never extended herself and constantly complained, neighbors were reluctant to spend time with her. Had she seen that she herself had control over her experiences, she might have made more of an effort to find people she enjoyed in the neighborhood.

Waiting for others to make us happy is a long and usually futile endeavor. It's no one else's job. Not your spouse, not your children, not your neighbors. Prince Charming (or Principal Charming) are not coming to your rescue. You must take charge of your own happiness. Commit to cultivating the qualities and taking the steps that will bring you happiness and satisfaction wherever you are. It won't happen accidently. It will happen because you make a commitment to your own happiness. And yet, perhaps ironically, much of your own happiness will come from your ability to care deeply about those around you.

KINDNESS AS AN ANTIDOTE
TO WHAT AILS YOU

In her recent study of the impact of kindness on health, Dr. Kelli Harding in *The Rabbit Effect* (2019) describes a scientific study of rabbits designed to measure the impact of high cholesterol foods on their health. All the rabbits in the study were fed the kinds of food known to cause arteries to clog. Eventually, the cholesterol levels of all the animals were measured and compared. As hypothesized, diet impacted all the rabbits almost identically. One group, however, despite the poor diet, continued to have low levels of cholesterol in their arteries. Scientists wrapped their brains around the unlikely outcome, trying to determine what could have caused one group alone to remain healthy despite what they thought was identical treatment.

Eventually they discovered that one kindhearted post-doctoral student, responsible for feeding that particular group, fed them exactly as had been prescribed, but also petted and played with them for a minute or two each day.

We know from numerous studies of orphaned infants that babies who are cuddled and touched are far healthier, both physically and emotionally, than babies who have been left to languish in their cribs with little human contact.

It seems obvious that rats, rabbits, humans, and probably every other living creature respond favorably to kindness and attention. Think about studies of plants that seem to show that plants respond favorably to being talked to or exposed to soothing music. Kindness is critical to our survival. But what we have failed to fully realize in the past is that being the recipient of kindness is not enough. We must also extend ourselves and be the giver of kindness to others to be emotionally and possibly, according to Dr. Harding, physically healthy.

Dr. Hardy postulates that kindness is an antidote to the inflammatory process. She emphasizes that positive interactions with others determine our overall health as much as our genes. As a matter of fact she suggests that medical care probably accounts for only about 20 percent of our health. The rest is a result of seeking out the kinds of happy and positive interactions with others that allow our bodies, flooded with endorphins, to heal and prosper.

> *Reflection: Is there a co-worker to whom I could show more kindness? How will I go about it?*

THE MIND AND BODY CONNECTION

Very few medical doctors focus on our social interactions or even our state of mind. While becoming more common, it is still the rare doctor who has the time or inclination to question his patients about their happiness, their social contacts, or the kind acts they give or receive. Indeed many doctors are so focused on one particular part of the body that they often ignore even our complete physical makeup, to say nothing of our emotional health.

My own doctor seems to allot about fifteen minutes to each patient. My doctor also spends most of our visit together asking me questions about my physical health and recording those responses on a computer screen, rarely even making eye contact with me.

We are not a collection of individual body parts. We are complex beings whose minds and bodies are intimately connected. A constant information exchange of physical and emotional interactions produces health or sickness. And those interactions are not limited to what's happening inside of ourselves, inside of our own bodies and minds. They are far more complex than even that. The interactions we have with others and the way we perceive those interactions also help to determine our level of happiness and our level of health.

As teachers we know that hurt people hurt people. Whether it be the abused child or the angry colleague, people who are hurting have difficulty being kind to others. Instead, they focus on themselves, their own pain, and their own needs. And sadly and certainly counterproductively, these are not people we are attracted to. These are not people we want to spend time with, despite the fact that these are the children and adults who need us the most.

All of us have trauma in our past; many of us are experiencing trauma in our present. No one skates through this world unscathed. When we experience the loss of a loved one, a divorce, or a serious injury, it is difficult to maintain a sense of gratitude and well-being. It is difficult to focus on caring about and being kind to those around us. The more trauma we experience, the more likely we are to be sick both physically and mentally.

Not all trauma rises to that level, however. Being ignored by a colleague, being reprimanded by a spouse, being spoken to harshly by a parent or a principal are all forms of trauma. Most of us experience some form of minor trauma every single day of our lives. So how do we maintain our positivity? How do we focus on self-care and, beyond that, contribute to the well-being of others? In other words, how do we navigate our imperfect world?

These are all critical questions. The way we answer them in philosophy and in practice will determine our health and happiness and contribute, for good or ill, to the lives of those around us.

REFERENCES

Brown, S. L., Nesse, R. M., Vinokur, A. D., & Smith, D. M. (2003). Providing social support may be more beneficial than receiving it: Results from a prospective study of mortality. *Psychological science, 14*(4), 320-327.

Caspi, A., Roberts, B. W., & Shiner, R. L. (2005). Personality development: Stability and change. *Annual Review of Psychology,* 56, 453-484.

Degges-White, S. (Mar. 28, 2016). The pursuit of happiness never ends well. *Psychology Today* https://www.psychol-ogytoday.com/us/blog/lifetime-connections/201603/the-pursuit-happiness-never-ends-well

DeNeve, K. M., & Cooper. (1998). The happy personality: A meta-analysis of 137 personality traits and subjective well-being. *Psychological Bulletin, 124*(2), 197-229.

Dweck, C. S. (2008). *Mindset: The new psychology of success.* Ballantine Books.

Fredrickson, B. L., & Losada, M. F. (2005). Positive affect and the complex dynamics of human flourishing. *The American Psychologist, 60*(7), 678-686.

Furnham, A. (2009). Locus of control and attribution style. In M. R. Leary, & R. H. Hoyle (Eds.), *Handbook of individual differences in social behavior* (pp. 274-287). Guilford Press.

Harding, K. (2019). *The rabbit effect: Live longer, happier, and healthier with the groundbreaking science of kindness.* Atria Books.

Lyubomirsky, S., King, L., & Diener, E. (2005). The benefits of frequent positive affect: Does happiness lead to success? *Psychological bulletin, 131* (6), 803-855.

Mogg, K., McNamara, J., Powys, M., Rawlinson, H., Seiffer, A., & Bradley, B. P. (2000). *Cognition and Emotion* 14(3), 375-399.

Maslow, A. H. (1943). A theory of human motivation. *Psychological Review, 50*(4), 370-396.

Philpot, V. D., Holliman, W. B., & Madonna, S., Jr. (1995). Self-statements, locus of control, and depression in predicting self-esteem. *Psychological reports, 76* (3) 1007-1010.

Ryan, R., & Deci, E. L. (2000). Self-determination theory and the facilitation of intrinsic motivation, social development, and well-being. *American Psychologist, 55*(1), 68-78.

Tod, D., Hardy, J., & Oliver, E. (2011). Effects of self-talk: A systematic review. *Journal of Sport and Exercise Psychology, 33*(5) 666-687.

CHAPTER 2

SCHOOL AND CLASSROOM CULTURE

Keep away from people who belittle your ambitions.
Small people always do that, but the really great can
make you feel that you too can become great.
—MARK TWAIN

Many years ago, I moved to a new state and began working as a first-grade teacher in an old, run-down school alongside many teachers who had been there for quite some time. I was overwhelmed with my move from teaching junior high to teaching first grade. Luckily, right next door was one of those "seasoned" teachers who often came into my classroom for a brief visit and to look around with her highly developed professional eye. I still remember her saying, "My what an interesting way to arrange your furniture. Now, how will THOSE children see the board?" and "Look at that daily schedule you've posted. How nice for the children. But did you forget that you'll need to insert library time?" My colleague was gentle and diplomatic, but her help and support meant the world to me, as I floundered with even the most basic managerial tasks required of a first-grade teacher.

My new mentor and I had very different philosophies about discipline, teaching reading, involving parents, etc. But she respected my expertise when it occasionally appeared, and we had wonderful discussions about the pros and cons of our various ideas and strategies. She was a milestone in my professional development, and I realized that much of our learning can occur in casual conversations in our own schools, if we are willing to learn from one another.

UNSPOKEN NORMS

Not all my colleagues were so helpful. Assisting a new teacher was not typically seen as a value or a priority. Understanding what I perceived as their aloofness took a bit of time. I kept thinking I was doing or saying something that was alienating other teachers. It took a while to get over my paranoia and realize that any new teacher would have received the same treatment from most of their colleagues here. New teachers in this school were typically ignored.

Every school has a culture that contains hidden norms. Those are the taken-for-granted rules of operation that are in play and nobody will hand you the playbook. Norms are usually not spoken but are observable if you watch carefully. And then again, sometimes you won't recognize them until you are hit over the head with one of them.

In this school, for example, in addition to the unwritten rule that nobody goes out of their way for a new faculty member, there was another unspoken rule that only griping could happen in the faculty room. Someone should have posted that rule for me since I both missed it and violated it.

A local newspaper reporter had visited my classroom to take pictures and write an article about a learning experience that was happening in my room. (I had called the paper, another violation of protocol that had eluded me.) The article was wonderful, and my students and I were so excited. The best part, however, was the serendipitous, oversized picture of one of the children who, probably more than any other child, needed to feel recognized and special. I cut out the article and the giant photo and danced to the faculty room at lunch time to share my joy with my colleagues. All conversation stopped as I posted the article on the bulletin board and rejoiced in the beautiful picture of my most insecure student. When I paused to take a breath and look around the room for the expected excitement, I was met with icy stares. After a few beats, their conversations resumed as if I had never been there.

The prevailing culture of that faculty, visited upon one another and the students each day, was a gloomy and negative appraisal of school life, no matter what there might have been to celebrate. And rest assured, whatever feeling tone predominates in a school is indeed shared with the students.

I think young people deserve better, but I think faculty and staff deserve better as well.

CHANGING SCHOOL CULTURE

After I retreated from the faculty room feeling deflated and embarrassed, a colleague with whom I had had few interactions to that point in time, came into my classroom with her lunch and asked if she might join me. "I know how you feel," she sympathized, "but know that there are some of us who would love to repair the negativity here. We should find one another, band together, and celebrate our work. Or we can do what others have done and transfer to another school. Personally, I think the kids here deserve better."

Nancy became my friend and my confidante. Others joined us. At Christmas time we decorated the hallways and pushed an old out-of-tune piano into the foyer where, before school began, we sang carols and invited students to join in. We designed schoolwide celebrations of student successes of all kinds. We worked with the librarian to implement cultural celebrations. We invited parents into our classes and found meaningful ways to use them and value their support. We got together for dinners and parties and invited the dour "Debbie Downers" amongst us to come as well. Most never came. Many continued to denigrate our attempts to change the school culture to one of caring and positivity and labeled our efforts as "fluff."

The culture *did* change, however. One day three or four years later, a new, young, enthusiastic teacher ran into the faculty room to show us a beautiful before-and-after sample of one student's writing. She was met with smiles and congratulations. That was the day I knew we had turned a corner.

And one more point about the faculty room if you please. Confidentiality. You have no right to discuss a child's problems with anyone who is not on the "need-to-know" list. Does your doctor tell his next patient about the unfortunate location of your boil? Confidentiality is part of professional ethics that is, sadly, commonly ignored. Who makes the "need-to-know" list? Possibly other teachers working with the child, parents, principal, etc. The question to ask is: "Can my student benefit from this person having access to this information?" If the answer is no, mums the word. Like the doctor, you are bound by professional ethics.

> Reflection: How would you describe the prevalent culture of your school? What steps might you take to improve the prevailing school culture?

CHANGING THE FACULTY ROOM CULTURE

So how does one person change the culture and feeling tone in a negatively charged faculty room? First, we need to understand and accept the need to vent. Teaching is hard work fraught with barriers and challenges to our best efforts. The faculty room is a safe place to unload and explode. So be it. The toxicity occurs when that's *all* that happens. Instead of a place of comradery and renewal, the faculty room becomes an arena of ugly competition for comparing the horrors of teaching, of students and, frequently, of parents. "You wanna know why George is such a piece of work? Have you met his mother?" This caliber of conversation is unprofessional and can quickly spiral out of control.

Acknowledging your own frustrations and that of your colleagues is the first step in changing the out-of-control faculty room negativity. Teachers need to vent. It's what happens next that matters. In a process known as *Appreciative Inquiry*, we learn about the art of the positive question. This inquiry is a skill that can be used with colleagues, students, family, and friends and is well worth practicing.

Instead of jumping into the fray with our own horror stories (and we all have them) of clueless parents and lazy students, we can provide uplifting support to the complaining, frustrated, and weary co-worker by framing an appreciative question to reverse the direction of the negativity spiral and tap into the wisdom and positivity of the group.

- So, how did you raise your own children to be responsible?
- What strategies have worked for you in the past?
- Have you ever had a success story working with a child like this one?

> *Reflection: Construct a positive question that you might use in the faculty room to change the tide of a negative conversation.*

By reframing the conversation with a positive question, we allow the other person to tap into their own strengths and successes in a way that helps them to adjust their frame of mind to one that is more positive and constructive.

Appreciative conversations like these promote comradery, positivity, and confidence in our abilities as teachers, while allowing us to learn from one another. Just the right question can make all the difference.

Every person has a core of strengths, wisdom, and successes that can be tapped and brought to the forefront with questions like,

- Why did you want to become a teacher?
- Is there a student in whose life you know you made a real difference?
- When have you felt real pride in your profession?
- Who has been your inspiration as a teacher?
- What makes you happy in your classroom?

Teachers sometimes retreat from the faculty room to protect themselves from the toxicity. While that may be a temporary solution, it does nothing for your very basic need for community, nor does it address the problem. If you need to "run for the hills" occasionally for your own sanity, do it. Remember, however, that this is your school, and you have a right to enjoy every part of it...even the faculty room.

CONNECTION AND COMMUNITY

Not so long ago, many people believed that happiness could only happen outside of the workplace. One of my colleagues loved to say, "I'm never happy at work. I'm here to teach. Period." She was suspicious of anyone who actually enjoyed their job, believing that they must not be *doing* their job. I never heard this woman laugh, and I never heard laughter come from her classroom. She also didn't believe that having an inviting environment in the classroom was part of her job. "If I had wanted to be an interior decorator, I would have." Consequently, there were no bulletin boards, no children's work on the walls, no color, and no happiness. Her sterile white classroom looked more like a hospital operating room than a classroom.

Not unlike my stern, unhappy colleague, my least favorite uncle now loves to bemoan the "snowflakes" among us who insist upon finding joy in their work. Uncle John is retired now, but he spent his life in a stifling hot mill doing a repetitious and mind-numbing job for forty years. No wonder he had the attitude he did. How lucky we are as teachers to work in a pleasant environment, doing work that we are educated to do, in ways that change lives and contribute to the welfare of our communities.

Let's face it, discouraged, grumpy people are no fun to work with, and they affect our schools in profoundly negative ways. Like the "one bad apple" in the barrel, they can impact the happiness and productivity of an entire organization. When someone is in the grip of strong negative emotions, they tend to see the world as a hostile place, and their hostility can be contagious and corruptive. Emotions at work matter, and attention to them is important.

We need to know that we matter and that we are cared about. We need to counteract negative feelings by bonding with positive people. We need to appreciate one another and feel comfortable expressing that appreciation. Considering that we spend at least forty hours a week at school, none of us can afford to work in an environment where we are ignored or unappreciated or surrounded by negativity. Friendships in the workplace matter.

> *Reflection: Is there someone with whom I can talk, laugh, and share worries and successes? Is there someone I look forward to seeing and talking to? How can I cultivate such a relationship?*

If we are to be proactive in finding friendships and happiness in our work lives, we really can't sit back and wait for others to come to us. It may be a long wait.

FINDING THE SUPPORT YOU NEED

When I moved to a position at the district office, I found everyone congenial. No one, however, initiated much more than a pleasant "Good morning" or "How's it going?" I missed my school friends and the happy relationships and connections I had taken for granted. I had previously thought of myself as a competent person, but suddenly, with no feedback or community support, I started to doubt my ability to do anything well and regretted my decision to change jobs. I was isolated and unhappy.

After weeks of trying to appear competent in a job I didn't yet understand, eating lunch by myself, and missing important meetings because I was out of the loop, I knew I would have to be proactive in my search for connections and friendships. I had been so impressed by one woman in my department who seemed articulate and well-liked.

With nothing to lose (but my dignity), I approached her one morning and suggested that we go to lunch together. I told her my positive impressions of her and admitted that I would very much like to get to know her better. She agreed to my humble but honest request, and we had a wonderful time at lunch. It felt good to admit my vulnerability and inability to connect with colleagues, to say nothing of establishing any real friendships. This woman, flattered I'm sure by my sincere admiration, became my mentor and biggest supporter. She made certain that I was included in social gatherings, checked on me before important meetings to make sure I knew where they were being held, and saved a seat for me anytime we were in the same room.

Most people would do the same. We're all so busy that we sometimes miss the signs of a colleague's struggles. We can't expect others to read our minds, and most of us have gotten so good at appearing self-sufficient, others would be amazed to know that we are far less sure of ourselves than we appear. If you need support, ask. You might be surprised at how caring most folks can be.

Conversely, we might try harder to really see our colleagues and anticipate the times when they might need additional support and caring. It takes little thought to realize that new teachers or teachers new to our school will need collegiality and friendship. Go out of your way to connect with these people. You can be sure it will be appreciated and may lead to mutually enjoyable relationships.

CLASSROOM CLIMATE

Teachers are not alone in needing to be valued, productive, and part of a supportive and safe environment. Students need those things as well. Safety is the most basic thing we can provide our children, and a child who doesn't feel safe will never feel valued or be able to be productive. So how can we guarantee each child's safety?

Awareness is critical. Keep your eyes and ears open for instances where a student is belittled, laughed at, excluded, or bullied. We all know that these things happen and happen frequently, but a teacher committed to creating a culture of respect and acceptance can lessen or eliminate this type of behavior, at least in his own classroom and among his own students, no matter where they happen to be. You need to spend some time on the playground and in the cafeteria. Watch and listen. You may be surprised.

Last year I conducted an anonymous survey in my college educational psychology class, asking how many of the students had been bullied at some point as school children. Twenty-five out of twenty-seven students reported having been bullied. We've all heard the "Boys will be boys" (hopefully that one died a miserable and painful death) and "Kids need to toughen up" and "Let them work it out for themselves." None of those thoughts help to create a safe environment for our students.

Perhaps counterintuitively, the class bully may need some help and support from you and the children. We know that frequently, bullying behavior is a result of mistreatment of some kind that is then perpetrated on others. You must never allow a student to bully others in any way, but that doesn't mean that you shouldn't help him or her to develop substitute strategies for their bullying behavior, and help the child find the satisfaction that comes from socially acceptable behavior. And, when you deem it appropriate, talk to the class about what strategies that the child is trying to learn and enlist their support.

The kids most harassed are often the weakest. Kindness and compassion must be taught and modeled. It must be threaded throughout the day in our conversations with our children. Good literature helps children to see the world from the other's point of view, helps them develop compassion, and helps them value qualities like kindness and concern. A good book followed by a thoughtful discussion is a wonderful way to regularly present the importance of kindness and compassion to children.

CLASS MEETINGS AND GOOD LITERATURE

Children love coming together for class meetings and love to have a great book read to them. Both these activities provide an opportunity to continue to teach appropriate behavior. Allow the children meeting time to talk about the success they are seeing among themselves in becoming a caring community. Children will happily report positive experiences and observations, and the child being praised becomes even more committed to improving his or her behavior.

Instead of having a classroom full of exasperated children because of having to witness another child's meltdowns or anger or other inappropriate behaviors, children become partners in helping one another to improve. There is nothing wrong with being honest with children who are seeing a child act inappropriately. "John is working hard to do better in expressing his feelings appropriately and we can all help him." Children will be thrilled to observe and report improvements, and hearing himself praised by peers, will probably be a wonderful new experience for this child.

There are so many great books that demonstrate kindness, caring, overcoming frustrations, making friends, and other social skills that are critical to a child's well-being. Avoid books that preach. Instead rely upon good literature that engages children, shows real struggles, paints people as they are, with faults and virtues. Check out Newberry winners, librarian recommendations, etc. Begin to collect your favorites. Many public libraries have regular book sales where books can be purchased for very little. Garage sales are a great way to enhance your collection and a great way to spend a relaxing couple of hours on a Saturday morning. Also, befriend those teachers close to retirement. Who knows? They may bequest their classroom library to you rather than having to store it in their garage for the next twenty years. Keep a list of books you would like to add to your collection and add to it as you discover new treasures.

Here are a few of my favorite books for children that can be used to spark discussions about positivity, empathy, and community:

- *How to Heal a Broken Wing* by Bob Graham
- *Stand Tall, Molly Lou Melon* by Patty Lovell
- *The Peace Book* by Todd Parr
- *Each Kindness* by Jacqueline Woodson
- *Can I Play Too* by Mo Willems
- *Stellaluna* by Janell Cannon
- *Chicken Sunday* by Patricia Polacco (actually anything by Patricia Polacco)
- *A Sick Day for Amos McGee* by Philip C. Stead

Reflection: What books would I like to have in my classroom library to create a healthy classroom climate?

I've seen teachers post a list of books they'd like to have donated to their classroom library on Facebook and have parents, friends, and family respond in no time. Be creative. Books don't have to cost you a fortune if you are creative and proactive. You might be surprised at how many people are willing to help you.

SPEAKING OF FACEBOOK

Be very, very, very careful about what you post on social media. Nothing is private!! I have seen teachers post highly personal information about themselves, use inappropriate language, and reveal way too much. If you must post, do it with the realization that your principal and parents may read it. Sadly, I've seen teachers talk about their frustrations, depression, anger, difficult students, etc. That is beyond unprofessional. To say nothing of the fact that it may come back to bite you.

REGULAR CONVERSATION

Every teacher should have regular conversations with their children that emphasize that their class is a family where everyone is valued and included. Talk about experiences on the playground. What happens and how do children feel who have no one to play with or who are excluded and bullied? Teach children to stand up for one another as classmates. Teach them strategies for dealing with any unkindness they may encounter outside. Let them know that you are there to listen and help them find ways to deal with difficult encounters. In those regular class meetings, children can report their success stories or ask for help, from you or from their classmates, in dealing with problems for which they haven't yet found solutions. You are not encouraging tattling. You are encouraging children to support one another as they develop individual skills to deal with unkindness, unfairness, or bullying.

One second-grade girl was confined to a wheelchair, and the children vied for the opportunity to push her to the lunchroom and outside for recesses. They considered it a privilege. They included her in their playground games and came up with ways she could participate in everything they were doing outside. This didn't happen automatically. It happened because a great teacher prompted those children to see another child as a part of their classroom family, worthy of respect and friendship.

Reflection: What steps will I take to be certain that school is a safe place for my students?

SATISFACTION

Being part of a hardworking, caring, and competent school community brings so much satisfaction. Working at a school where teachers care about one another and work together to create a safe, positive, and effective learning environment for students creates personal satisfaction and a sense that your work matters. Implicit in this environment is one's personal responsibility to promote a school culture of positivity and caring. As Mother Teresa enjoined, "Be the change you wish to see."

REFERENCES

Baumeister, R. & Leary, M. R. (1995). The need to belong: Desire for interpersonal attachments as a fundamental human motivation. *Psychological Bulletin, 117,* 497–529.

Bourdieu, P. (1991). *Language and symbolic power.* Harvard University Press.

Brubacher, J. W., Case, C. W., & Regan, T. G. (1994). *Becoming a reflective educator.* Corwin Press.

Bruner, J. (1996). *The culture of education.* Harvard University Press.

Cadmus, F. (2012). Happiness at work: Rules for employee satisfaction and engagement;

Cornell law faculty publications: Paper 654., 56, 453–484.

Christensen, E., Rossi, T., Hunter, L., & Tinning, R. (2018). Entering the field: beginning teachers' positioning experiences of the staffroom. *Sport, Education and Society* 23(1), 40–52.

Novak, J. M. (1992). *Advancing invitational thinking.* Caddo Gapp Press.

Stoll, L. (1998). School Culture: Black hole or fertile garden for school improvement in School Culture J. Prosser (Ed.) Paul Chapman.

Whitney, D., & Trosten-Bloom, A. (2003). *The power of appreciative inquiry.* Berrett-Koehler Publishers.

CHAPTER THREE

BONDING WITH PARENTS

It's a funny thing about mothers and fathers. Even when their own child is the most disgusting little blister you could ever imagine, they still think that he or she is wonderful.
—RONALD DAHL

Ronald Dahl knew what he was talking about and so do you, especially if you've had one of those "disgusting little blisters" in your classroom. It's pretty universal, however, that no parent will ever believe that his child could be the problem. One of my teacher friends set up a conference with little Jacob's parents because he was having so much difficulty focusing and paying attention. After listening attentively, the parent announced that the problem was probably that the teacher wasn't entertaining enough. (Sigh.) I know parental denial to be true, not because I've encountered so many defensive or naive parents (which I have), but because I too am a parent.

When my daughter Elaina's principal called to tell me that Elaina would be in detention for the next week because she had been throwing rocks at a passing train, I was horrified. Not because of Elaina's actions, but because the principal could believe, for even one moment, that my precious little daughter could have done such a thing. I was filled with righteous indignation. No plethora of eyewitnesses would convince me. Elaina was in the third grade. Elaina knew better. Elaina had me for a parent, and I certainly had taught her better than that. Of course I never specifically mentioned not throwing rocks at passing trains to her, but surely I didn't need to. I had taught her about respecting property, about being trustworthy, and about setting an example for other children who could not possibly have been parented as well as Elaina had. Trains never came up.

Looking back, I suppose I should have been more specific, but what parent can anticipate every transgression. When the principal produced a photo on her phone of Elaina's pitching arm poised in the air as a train went by, bolstered by three or four eye-witnesses, I finally became a believer. I had taught my children, Elaina included, never to lie and always take responsibility for any errors in judgment they might make. By errors in judgment I imagined their forgetting to bring a pencil to class or being a minute or two late after recess because they were helping an unfortunate student gather their lost belongings from beneath the swing set. My mind never once wandered to egregious offenses like intentionally damaging public property while endangering the lives of others.

Eventually I learned that Elaina and my other three children were capable of almost anything, including not being truthful. Oh alright, outright lying. I learned to have faith in the principal, the teachers, tattling neighbors, and everyone else who came to me with horror stories about my children. That's not to say that I was raising disgusting little blisters, but let's face it, all of us are capable of raising blisters and even being blisters now and again. I know I am.

If parents are overly protective of their children, it usually means that their eyes have not yet been opened. They are trusting souls convinced that their good parenting is all that's required for raising perfect children. Be gentle. Forgive them. They will learn.

PARENTS AS ALLIES

Parents are not the enemy. Parents are the reason you have a job. They provide the raw materials. Nevertheless, unhappy, complaining parents can kill your joy faster than a rampant case of poison ivy. Like students, they can smell your fear, so you must be brave. "Fake it 'til you make it" is a good motto. Pretend you're at ease with parents and soon you will be if, and only if, you initiate contact in a positive way.

I advised my teachers to try something that was successful for me year after year. I'll warn you now that it's time intensive but, in the long run, it will make your work so much happier and give you instant credibility with parents. Here it is:

The minute you receive your class list at the beginning of the year set up a timetable to phone the parents of each child on that list. And you must do it before school starts. Your conversation will go something like this,

Hello, Mr. Jones,

This is Sandy Petersen. I'm Jason's new teacher. I'm wondering if you have just a few minutes for a chat. I'd like to get to know a bit about Jason before the school year begins and, since you know him better than anyone, I thought it would be nice to get to know you.

Unless their house is on fire, every parent will stop whatever they're doing. Curiosity and novelty will get the best of them, and they'll tell you that this is a fine time for a chat.

And so, you continue,

Tell me a little about Jason. What does he like to do? What are his strengths and best qualities? What would you like to see him accomplish this year?

And you're off and running.

I have made this phone call hundreds of times, and by the end of the conversation, the parent has become a friend and ally, mostly because no other teacher has ever contacted them this way. Teachers contact parents when there's a problem, not to consult them or to invite the parent into their child's educational experience.

Some parents, maybe most, will tell you that their child enjoys school, does well, and excels in one thing or another. Take notes. There is an equally important purpose to this call and that is to gather meaningful information that will help you meet the needs of each child. At the first individual parent teacher conference, you pull out your notes, and discuss the items parents mentioned in their phone call. That's impressive and lets them know that you listened and truly valued their input.

Other calls will take more time. Some parents will pour out their heart telling you about the bad experiences their child has had in school. He's not learning; other children don't like him; they can't get him to even go to school some days, etc. You need to know this. You need to talk about a preliminary action plan to help this child and support this frantic parent. You need to assure the parent, and indeed all the parents, that you will do everything in your power to make the upcoming year a happy and successful one for their student. And you really are off to a great start because you have an individual profile on each student and have established a bond with each parent.

If the thought of all those personal phone calls causes big balls of sweat to form on your forehead, you can accomplish *almost* the same thing by sending a letter and survey home to the parents. If your principal will spring for the postage, it's always nice to send this kind of survey before you meet the kids. By the way, an email is less personal but better than nothing. Your letter might look something like this:

SAMPLE LETTER BEFORE THE
START OF THE SCHOOL YEAR

Dear _____ ,

My name is Mr. Smith and I will be Johnny's third grade teacher this year. I'm delighted to have your child in my class, and I take my responsibilities as a teacher most seriously. My goal is to ensure that this is the best school year your child has ever had and that he or she grows by leaps and bounds.

Having a partnership with you will add value to the school experience this year, and I hope to have a wonderful relationship with you as well as with your child. Together we can optimize the schoolyear.

Because I know that you know more about your child than anyone else, I would like to ask you a few questions to help me get the year started right. Too often teachers spend valuable time learning about a child's strengths and needs when a simple communication with the parents could have easily provided that information before the school year has even begun.

In that spirit, would you take a few minutes to fill in the attached survey.

If you would rather call me, you are certainly welcome to do that. I can be reached at _____ from 3:30 until 5:00 Monday through Friday.

Most sincerely,

(Take the time to hand sign the letter).

John Smith

What questions would you like to ask in the survey? What would be valuable information for you? Try to focus on what matters to you and keep the survey brief, providing an option for additional information if the parent so desires.

Here is an example of a survey that you might want to use as a template:

Your child's name _____

Your name _____

What do you see as your child's strengths and best qualities?

What would you like to see your child accomplish this year?

Are there particular concerns you have?

What should I know about your child before the schoolyear begins?

If you would like to provide additional information, please feel free. Attach additional sheets if you like.

Please return this in the enclosed, stamped and addressed envelope at your convenience. I look forward to meeting you in person very soon.

Now you've started off on a good foot with the parents. Be aware that this is not just a PR stunt of some sort. The information you glean will be of great value to you. Take notes during your phone calls or save the written surveys and keep a file on each child. Review that file before you meet parents for the first time, so that you can mention their remarks and concerns and tell them how you plan to address them. Parents need to know that you have listened and value their input.

Don't stop with this first communication. Plan to send home regular happy notes or periodic positive phone calls to stay in touch with parents and celebrate the good things their child has done. You can set a goal to have a certain number of contacts each week and keep track so that you stay in contact with the parents or guardians of every child in your class. You can also find an assortment of free-for-the taking certificates online. Print them and keep a stash in your desk so that these communications are quick and easy. Just be sure to personalize them, and parents and children will be thrilled. Did Johnny master his spelling list this week? Help a classmate? Improve his time management? Remember his homework? No accomplishment is too small to celebrate, and every communication tells a parent how much you care about their child.

WHEN THERE'S A PROBLEM

Parents deserve to know what's going on with their child at school. Keeping information from them because you dread making that phone call is unfair and unprofessional. Would you like it if your child's dentist kept his rotting molar a secret from you?

That phone call will be far easier because you have already made positive contacts with the parent. One contact, however, isn't enough. Keep parents informed with a monthly parent newsletter, a classroom website, and, of course, with those frequent personal notes identifying a specific accomplishment their child has made. Remember, it need not be earth shattering, just honest and sincere.

We've been working on coming in from recess just as soon as the bell rings, and Johnny did it today!

Once again, I noticed Lisa including one of the often left out children in her game. She always demonstrates such kindness.

Pablo has mastered those pesky nine times tables. Wahoo!

These quick notes can mean the world to a parent while letting them know how much you value their child. Little things really do mean a lot.

Once upon a time, as was my custom as a principal, I greeted children at the front door as they entered the building each morning. We exchanged high fives, encouraging words, and an occasional hug. One morning a little boy I had never noticed before walked in, and I engaged him in a conversation.

"You gonna have a great day today?" I asked and he was

off and running, regaling me with descriptions of the science projects they were working on in his fourth-grade class and the jump shot he would definitely make today at recess. He wore oversized glasses that made his eyes disconcertingly large and that needed to be pushed up to the top of his button nose every ten seconds or so. The nose, by the way, was running, in a most unfortunate and yellow manner. I surreptitiously handed him a tissue as he continued to ramble on excitedly. This little guy's enthusiasm for life knew no bounds, nor did his vocabulary. I finally walked with him to his classroom because it seemed easier than stopping his flow of words.

When all the students were in their classes and the building quieted, I found this little boy's home phone number and gave his folks a call to tell them what a delightful child they had produced and how impressed I was with his enthusiasm, to say nothing of his vocabulary.

It was his mother who answered the phone, and after I introduced myself and told her about my delightful visit with her son, there was a long pause. At first, I thought we had been disconnected, and then she said in an irritated voice,

Is this a joke?

I was as taken aback as she must have been by my call.

No. Of course not. I was so impressed and delighted by your child and just wanted to tell you about it.

When this mom was convinced that I was indeed the principal and that my praise of her son was sincere, she told me that over the years she had many calls from the school, but none of them, until today, had been positive. All she had ever heard was that her son talked too much, disrupted the class, couldn't sit still, etc. One teacher had even suggested that Ritalin might be in order. (I hope that teacher had an MD as well as a teaching license, since teachers are not authorized to prescribe medication.)

As we said goodbye, my happy mood had disappeared. How sad that this child had not been appreciated. How many other little antsy and excitable children (and their parents) had been made to feel that there was something wrong with them and that they were not valued and appreciated by their teacher.

The excitable, talkative, can't-keep-her-hands-to-herself child is sometimes seen as a disruptor to a teacher's well-planned lesson. They make it difficult to adhere to that all important, carefully posted daily schedule (okay, that's sarcasm). Critical time is wasted responding to their many comments and questions, reminding them to sit down, to give someone else a turn, to stop eating their crayons, etc. I know. I've been frustrated, too. But what if we celebrated this child, saw their curiosity and conversations as a joyful celebration of young minds exploring a world that is wonderful and new. Of course, we must help them regulate their behavior, but that is far different than crushing their spirits and complaining to their parents. You are the professional. Let this child know how happy you are about their love of learning and how, together, you will encourage others in the class to share *their* understandings and questions as well.

One cranky kindergarten teacher in our school repeatedly brought a little girl to my office where she unceremoniously dumped her with the admonition, "You deal with her. I can't take it anymore." One day when this teacher seemed not quite as cranky as usual, I dared ask for specifics about little Mary Beth's behavior. Her sins? "She talks and she won't sit down." Excuse me? Do we really want 5 year olds to be silent, and why in the world would a five-year-old want to sit still?

This is the reason that so many children enter kindergarten filled with bubbly joy and boundless curiosity and leave fifth or sixth grade stooped over and subdued, hating everything about the unnatural condition known as "school."

Lest you think that all teachers are joyless, merciless taskmasters, let me be clear that I have worked with far more dedicated and enthusiastic teachers than the few perennially grumpy who really should be counseled into a different career path. By the way, if you ever decide to become a principal, counseling some teachers out of the profession will be part of your job description and should be taken seriously.

INVITATIONAL EDUCATION

William Purkey, a great educator and one of my heroes, writes about what he has termed *Invitational Education*. He identifies our level of behavior toward others, children and parents, according to four categories worth thinking about.

Intentionally Disinviting

The teacher knows he is being unwelcoming and cold, but really doesn't care. I don't know anyone who actually falls into this category, but I suppose it happens.

Unintentionally Disinviting

Okay. We've all been guilty of this one. We don't mean to be rude or dismissive, but we are. We get tired or overworked or overwhelmed and aren't thinking about how we are coming across to others. Sometimes we hurt feelings in this mode. It's unintentional, but it can still sting and damage relationships.

Unintentionally Inviting

These are the teachers we know who are just naturally sunny and pleasant. They make everyone, students, parents, and colleagues feel welcome and valued without really needing to give it much thought. It's just who they are.

Intentionally Inviting

This is where we all strive to be. By being intentional in our desire we can come that much closer to operating at this level as often as possible. The bottom line is that we cannot expect our students to be kind and courteous to others unless we strive to model that behavior ourselves.

We all tell our students to be kind. But what does that actually look and sound like? Remind yourself of the goal to be intentionally inviting and practice it as much as you can without giving yourself a giant Excedrin headache. Sometimes, even the best of us drop down a level or two!

INVITING PARENTS TO YOUR CLASS

How inviting are you? Do you encourage parents to visit or to volunteer in your class? Some teachers are deathly afraid of being observed. (That ugly inferiority complex rears its head yet again.) But to get over that reluctance, you need to plunge in and do it. Parents are free aides. Who doesn't need help in their classroom?

So how do you get started with a parent volunteer program? First, realize that it IS a program. You must plan ahead for the most effective use of parent volunteers. Nothing makes a parent feel more useless and unappreciated than walking into a classroom where the teacher announces., "Oh, I forgot you were coming…geez what can I give you to do?" Parent volunteers are not impositions; they are resources. Plan for their most effective use and make them part of your program. If you need something cut out or other mindless tasks, please save that to send home to parents who can't come to the school but would like to help in some small way. They can watch *Dancing with the Stars* and cut simultaneously. Those willing to come to your classroom need to be engaged in meaningful ways if you expect them to continue to be there on a regular basis. So,

Step One: Decide what your parent volunteers can do to support teaching and learning.

When I taught first grade, I prepared a folder for each child that included a current book on their individual reading level. The folders were placed at a table with one ADULT- sized and one child's chair, and parents came in at a preassigned time during my Language Arts block to listen to individual children read. The adult came into the classroom, went to their spot, selected the top file folder, and called that child's name. Kids loved it. They got to read with somebody's mom or dad or grandparent. They were getting extra individualized reading practice, something I didn't have the time for, while I worked with other children. After they had read to the volunteer, that file went to the bottom of the stack. Notice I'm not asking parents to teach. They aren't trained. Nor am I asking them to run off papers. That's not why they're there. Use them efficiently. Plan your program before you ever invite a parent to come in.

> *Reflection: How can I most effectively use parents in my classroom? How can I set things up to be efficient and valuable for children?*

Step Two: Invite volunteers.

Now that you have a plan, you can send out the message that you are looking for volunteers. Give them options for how often they would be expected to be there. Let them know you will train them in their job requirements and that you sincerely welcome their presence. Some volunteers may be able to come once or twice during a week, others once a month. Also provide an option for parents who can't come in but would be willing to do some clerical kinds of work at home. This is free labor! Whenever I hear a teacher bemoan their inability to keep up with all the work required, I ask them if they are using volunteers. Here's an idea to get you started:

SAMPLE VOLUNTEER INVITATION

Dear Parents,

I would welcome your help in our classroom if you are willing and able. I know that many of you hold down jobs or have other commitments that would make that impossible (but don't worry, I have jobs for you, as well!)

☐ I could help in the classroom on a regular basis.

☐ Weekly ☐ Bi-weekly ☐ Monthly

☐ I can't come in but I could do some work at home.

☐ I have a special talent or interest that I could share with the class.

Please describe and let me know when you might be available.

☐ I could help out now and again for a special occasion (field trips, parties, projects)

☐ No can do. Maybe next year.

Your Name _____

Preferred Contact Information _____

Thank you!

Step Three: Train your volunteers.

Invite all your volunteers to a meeting, where you introduce them to one another and give them an opportunity to get acquainted. You're building community, remember? Then show and tell them exactly what will be expected of them when they come in to volunteer. They should be able to go straight to work without talking to you at all. In this meeting, be sure to stress confidentiality. Just like Las Vegas, what they see or hear in the classroom, stays in the classroom. Their next-door neighbor doesn't need to know that little Mikey doesn't read as well as little Fred.

> *Reflection: What do I see as the most important points to cover in the initial volunteer training meeting?*

Step Four: Develop a monthly schedule to share with volunteers.. People's availability will change, so know that you will need to produce a schedule each month. You can cut down on your secretarial workload by assigning this job to one of your homebound volunteers. These folks can be invaluable in cutting, pasting, making phone calls, tracking down donations, rounding up toilet paper tubes, shoe boxes, and a variety of other time-consuming tasks. Home volunteers get a monthly schedule as well.

Be sure to include every person who volunteers, and don't overburden anyone. Parents who help you, in even small ways, are invested in your classroom, and that's exactly what you want.

Step Five: Send personal thank you notes periodically.
Saying thank you is just polite and will mean the world to your parents.

OTHER SOURCES OF VOLUNTEERS

What if enough parents don't volunteer to work in the classroom? Realistically, we know that many families have two parents who are working or just one parent in the home. There are other sources of volunteers, however, and one of the best is grandparents. Working through your parents, compile a list of grandparents and contact them. Many retired folks are looking for meaningful volunteer work, and you are just the person to provide it for them. If there is a college nearby, education students may be interested in working with you in the classroom for practical experience. Contact the chair of the education department. Some high schools have identified future teachers and will release them to you, as well.

The rules are the same. Have definite, meaningful volunteer program in place, train your volunteers, work around their schedules, and thank them sincerely and profusely.

GETTING OVER YOUR STAGE FRIGHT

Once you have well-trained volunteers in your classroom, you will quickly learn to go about your business as they go about theirs, and your reluctance to have people in your classroom will vanish. It will just be a part of business as usual. This working environment will prepare you (okay, at least a little bit) for your evaluation visits from the principal and will certainly help you to feel more comfortable when other teachers ask if they might come and watch how your volunteer program works. Nothing improves teaching quite as much as excellent teachers coming into one another's classrooms to pick up new ideas and teaching strategies.

No one expects you to be perfect, but when your parents and grandparents observe the difficulty and complexity of teaching a room full of diverse kids, they will develop a new-found appreciation for you. Hey, they'll love you. Remember that, for most of them, their only experiences in school were many years ago as students. The world looks very different when an *adult* has the opportunity to watch teachers in action.

THE DIFFICULT PARENT

One of my most satisfying jobs was working in a large, year-round school, first as a teacher and later as the principal. The school was in a high poverty area with trailer courts and government-subsidized apartment houses. Children moved frequently, which sometimes allowed us only a brief time to know them and teach them. That was the downside. The upside was that the school was full of teachers who loved working with children and families in this lower socioeconomic bracket. They knew how much they could change a child's outlook with caring and high expectations, and they were up to the challenge. I will never forget the sight of two special education teachers running after the garbage truck to give the garbage collector dad an opportunity to sign the necessary permission form so that his son could be tested for special services.

Nevertheless, I spent a goodly amount of time meeting with disgruntled parents. When the price of a lunch ticket went up, many parents were irate. If a teacher wanted children to buy a poster board for a project, it could be a hardship for parents who were quick to call me or show up in my office to complain vociferously. Some parents wanted their children to stay at school until six o'clock or later when the parents left work and could pick them up. Not every parent had a phone, so some calls were impossible. Not every home had a computer, so email correspondence was worthless. Children often came to school sick because there was no money for either a doctor or a babysitter. Some parents viewed school and teachers as the enemy, assuming they and their children were being judged for perceived parental shortcomings. I learned from those amazing teachers that our job is to teach, never to judge.

I learned from angry parents that we must spend more time understanding the issues that faced them. Often, I sat across from...and then next to... a parent who was worried, frustrated, and stressed, not because of what the school was doing, but because of terrible issues they were facing elsewhere. I saw parents holding down multiple jobs and feeling inadequate because they could not spend more time with their children. I visited with single parents...moms and sometimes dads...who depended upon school breakfasts and lunches to feed their children. In my many years as an educator, I did meet parents who were terrible at parenting, who were mean and abusive, and who were negligent. But I never met a parent who didn't love his child. That sounds like such a contradiction, but, in my experience, it was true. They may have been clueless as to how to raise children in a healthy environment, but they always cared and wished they could be better.

Parents, angry at a teacher for some perceived or actual grievance, almost always forgave when they spent time with the teacher and realized how much that teacher cared about their child. We are all imperfect. Many bonds were formed among parents and school personnel when we acknowledged that we are all simply trying our best and sometimes falling short.

The psychologist Erich Fromm said, *"A mother's love is peace. It need not be acquired, it need not be deserved."* The same can and must be said of a teacher's love. Every child must know with certainty that you love them unconditionally and that you value them for who they are. While others may see their faults, you see their strengths and their potential, and you will do all in your power, together with their parents, to help them become all they can and want to be.

YA CAN'T WIN 'EM ALL

Now and again a parent comes along who cannot be satisfied. They are angry at you for some real or imagined failing and will not be reasonable. All you can do is try...and then try not to let it get you down. You are not a failure because you can't please all the people all the time. You are a human being living in a human world that just isn't always fair.

There are some steps you can take in conflict situations, and believe me, you'll have those situations no matter how saintly you may be. Try these and, if they don't work, be ready to live the Serenity Prayer:

> *God grant me the serenity to accept the things*
> *I cannot change. Courage to change the things*
> *I can. And wisdom to know the difference.*

Very few teachers have been trained in conflict resolution strategies, but it's a skill that you will need to have sooner or later. I wish it were part of every teacher education program. What you learn about conflict resolution can help you in your day-to-day world, not just with parents but with co-workers, spouses, teenagers, surly clerks, and anyone else you find yourself in contact with. Effective conflict management will lower your stress and help you deal with life's big and little annoyances in a positive and (usually) effective way.

SO HOW CAN YOU DEAL WITH THE ANGRY PARENT?

Step One: Listen

Before you contradict, and you will be SO tempted, listen carefully to what the parent has to say. Give them a chance to get it all out before you say a word. Often, as they're winding down you'll hear them become more reasonable. "Well, I'm sure that's not exactly what happened, but that's how little Freddie told it to me" or "You've always been fair before, so I don't understand how this could have happened." Don't say anything until they are completely finished with whatever they've come to say to you.

While they're talking, be mindful of what your body is saying. Uncross your arms, lean slightly forward, and give a slow slight nod occasionally to encourage them to keep going. Keep your face as neutral as possible. Resist the urge to defend yourself or, just as infuriating to the injured party, repeat what they're saying to you in the manner in which we've been taught to address opponents. "I see…I hear you say that…" Everyone knows this technique, and over the years it has become trite and condescending. Say nothing. Stay in neutral. Wait for the person to completely wind down. Sometimes, just when you think they're finished, you'll hear, "And another thing…" so wait until they're worn out and completely finished.

Can you simply argue and defend yourself? Of course, but being right is the booby prize. Your bigger goal is to mend and then rebuild a relationship with the parent, for the sake of the child.

Step Two: Apologize
What? I didn't do anything wrong! I didn't do what the person is accusing me of. Why should I apologize? For what? You apologize for their upset and/or for the child's upset.

I'm so sorry this happened.

I'm so sorry this is what you heard.

I'm so sorry you've been so upset.

I'm so sorry that you and little Freddie have been upset by this.

Even if the accusations are completely ridiculous, untrue, or half true, the fact remains that this person felt it upsetting enough to take time away from their life to come to the school to confront you. They are upset, and that's too bad. Apologize for their upset. Nothing diffuses anger like a gentle "I'm so sorry."

Step Three: Join Forces

How do you join forces with the parent to eliminate an adversarial confrontation and move you both to the same side of the issue? Be prepared with a statement that subtly moves you from opponents to teammates. Try one of these or, better yet, write your own sentences that are natural and comfortable for you to use.

We both care about little Freddie and would never want him to feel this way.

It means a lot to me to work with you, and I would not want to harm our relationship.

I know that if we work together we can fix this problem.

> *Reflection: Write one or two statements that feel natural to you to use to join forces with a parent.*

Step Four: Clarify

Here's where you explain what you actually saw, heard, or did. Now is your time to clarify the situation without calling little Freddie a liar. Remember that perception is everything.

Oh wow, I can see now how Freddie might have interpreted it that way. Here's how I saw it.

Just don't try to wiggle out of something you did that really was wrong. Own up. That's what we expect our students to do and, difficult though it may be, when we're wrong, we need to say so and apologize for it.

Step Five: Plan for Follow-up

How can we remedy the situation together? How and when can we communicate again to be sure we're on track? A regular phone call? A weekly note home? Another meeting? Whatever you decide to do, be absolutely certain to follow through.

Step Six: Thank the Parent for Coming In

This is the easy step because by this point in the meeting you will be profoundly grateful that you've reached the end and probably be awash with gratitude! Here are some ideas for the thank you step.

I might never have known about this issue if you hadn't taken the time to call it to my attention. Thank you.

I'm so grateful to work with such a caring parent. Thank you for coming in.

No one enjoys conflict, and I'm grateful that you came to see me no matter how difficult it might have been. Thank you.

Do you want to be right or do you want to be happy? Working with parents, even those who seem unreasonable, is a far simpler road in the long run and it is certainly the road that is best for children. Children are happier and more secure when they know that their parents and their teacher work together and have a relationship based on mutual respect.

WHEN NO IS THE RIGHT ANSWER

But what happens when you *can't* work with a parent because their request or demands are unreasonable or not in the best interests of children? There are times when you absolutely cannot accommodate a parent's request or agree to their demands and, in those cases, your response must be a firm NO.

- If you are being asked to violate school policy, the answer is no.
- If you are asked to violate your own carefully thought out, professional policy that you know is in the best interests of your students, the answer is no.
- If you are asked to violate your personal or professional ethics, the answer is no.

That's often easier said than done and requires the ability to be firm while remaining as positive as possible.

So how do you go about saying no? The easiest way is to sandwich your "no" between an empathy statement and an alternative.

Suppose, for example, a parent dislikes a book on the library shelf and wants it removed. As always, listen carefully and don't interrupt. Then do three things:

1. Empathize with the request.
   Yes, I can see why that might be very important to you. I want every child to be exposed to the best literature, too.

2. Say no. Be firm and unequivocal.
   However, that's not a book we would remove from the shelves. It's won a number of awards, and many parents are eager to have their children read it.

3. Give them an alternative.
   As George's parent, you have a right to request that HE not read that book and that I absolutely can do that for you. You can also contact the library specialists at the district office to voice your concerns.

You may want to find out in advance how your district handles objections to books. In many districts, parents with concerns can fill out a form that is then taken to a panel at the district level for a final decision. This is an issue that will inevitably come up for you, but the good news is it's one you can prepare for by knowing your district's policy. Handing things off to your principal or to district administrators is not passing the buck *if* you have done your due diligence. Some decisions are just beyond your pay grade.

Here's another example that you might think about before it happens.

A parent comes to you, angry about a grade you have given to their child and wants you to change it. This is one of those times when your professional ethics and decision making come into question. Unless you have inadvertently given the wrong grade, in which case you apologize and correct it, the answer must be no. Listen carefully and respectfully to what the parent has to say and then use the same steps:

1. Empathize with the request.
   We always want our children to do well. It's upsetting when they come home with a poor grade.

2. Say no.
   I don't change grades. I'd be happy though to share with you exactly why little Leroy earned this grade. Let's look at the work and the scores he's earned this semester. His grade has been carefully calculated and is in place to inform you of his progress. To change it would be dishonest on my part.

3. Give them an alternative.
   What we can do, however, is to make sure that Leroy works hard enough next semester to improve this grade. Here's how you can help, and here's what we might do.

Perhaps you've forgotten that Leroy should be bringing a form from me each week indicating his scores that week and where he needs practice. I suspect those aren't making it home, or the grade might not have been so surprising to you. If you will contact me any time you don't see that report, I'll share that information with you directly. Another option might be for you to sign the weekly report and send it back. Which would work better for you?

It is never pleasant to have to say no to a parent, but it is sometimes necessary. You are the professional, and you have a right to make decisions that are in the best interests of children. When you can accommodate parents' requests, and they are reasonable, try to do that. Caring about and supporting our parents is almost as important as doing that for our students. Cultivate positive relationships with parents and they will *almost* always support you. Do your best and stick to your guns when you must. Dealing repeatedly with disruptive, demanding, or unreasonable parents is not part of your job responsibility. Turn that over to your principal.

Just remember that you can't win 'em all, no matter how much you care and how hard you try.

REFERENCES

Borisoff, D. & Victor, D. A. (1998). *Conflict management* (2nd ed.) Allyn & Bacon.

Botrie, M. & Wenger, P. (1992). *Teachers and parents together.* Pembroke Publishers.

Fromm, E. S. (1956). *The art of loving.* Harper.

Kerpen, D. (2016). *The art of people: 11 simple people skills that will get you everything you want.* Broadway Business.

Purkey, W. W., & Novak. J. M. (2016). *Fundamentals of invitational education.* The International Alliance for Invitational Education.

Simmons, S. J. (2020). *Root narrative theory and conflict resolution: Power, justice and values.* Routledge.

Toropov, B. (1997). *The art and skill of dealing with people.* Prentice Hall.

Zadeh, A. A. (2017). *The forgotten art of love: What love means and why it matters.* New World Library.

CHAPTER FOUR

CLASSROOM MANAGEMENT

I had my patience tested. I'm negative.
—UNKNOWN

The art of classroom management is paramount no matter how many years you've been teaching, and most new teachers are hugely concerned about this...as are their principals. An out-of-control class is devastating and signals that a teacher is incapable, and children are not learning. No wonder new teachers perseverate on this aspect of their job. Yet, as teachers master some of the elements of classroom management, they gradually become more focused on delivery of instruction and student learning and gradually find their feelings of disappointment transforming into feelings of competence and peace.

More teachers probably leave the profession because

of their inability to manage the behavior of their students than for any other reason. "Manage" implies a control over the children that is perhaps why some teachers fail. It is exhausting to be constantly in control. Children must have an internal desire to be on their best behavior. I can hear the nay-sayers now. "Well, that will never happen." For 95 percent of your children, it can and will happen if you set up your classroom in a way that encourages children to do and be their best. So, how to begin?

BEGIN ON DAY ONE.

You've already spoken with parents, so you know quite a bit about each of your students before they walk into your classroom on that first day of school. The children are excited to meet you. They may know you by reputation or not at all. Their parents have mentioned your phone call, so they're aware that there is already a teacher-parent pipeline in place. Today is the honeymoon. Take advantage of that by setting the tone for classroom expectations.

Everyone loves a fresh start and children are no exception. This is a new day for them. A clean slate. A chance to be the very best they can be in the positive and uplifting environment you create together. Most children will be nervous. Some will be skeptical. Others may feel a sense of relief if, indeed, their poor reputation does not carry over into this class.

Proximity is a great advantage in building rapport. Bring the children closer to you. You should have a corner of your classroom where children can gather for a story or a class meeting. Being in proximity with your students subtly changes the relationship to one of enhanced intimacy. The earlier in the day you have this first meeting, the better. The honeymoon period doesn't last long! Children will usually be quiet and receptive, eager to hear what you are going to say. I cannot overemphasize the importance of these first remarks. They should go something like this:

I'm so very glad to see each one of you.

If you are okay with white lies, and not afraid that your nose will grow, tell them that you selected each one of them individually to be in your class. (I love that touch, but I don't want to compromise your values.)

Each of you is different. Some of you are great readers; some not. Some are good at math; others not so much. Some love sports or art; others aren't very good.

The point you're making here is that you have no expectations for everyone to be great at everything. Then you let them know that it doesn't matter where they are at the beginning of the year. Each of them will learn and be successful. I tell them about my own children, now grown. One walked at nine months and one didn't walk until fifteen months. It doesn't matter. They're both good walkers now. Well phrased, this pep talk brings incredible relief to the child who has learned to feel as if everyone is better at learning than she is.

I don't care where you are as we get started on our year together. My job is to help you learn and teach you in a way that will make that happen. If I teach something that you don't understand, I'll teach it in a different way. If you still don't understand, I'll teach it in still another way. We'll keep going until you get it. That's what teachers do.

It doesn't hurt, here, to talk about an actual experience you've had yourself, where learning something proved to be difficult for you.

Your next talking point is incredibly important for successful classroom management. Tell the students,

I want you to know that in this classroom you will never be embarrassed, and you will always be respected. That's the way I will treat you, and I expect that you will treat me the same way. "Respect" is our motto. It is important that you respect each one of your classmates as well. We respect one another and we take care of one another. We are never rude. How does that sound to you?

At this point students will wholeheartedly agree that this is the way to live! (Always easier said than done, of course.)

You are building relationships, setting expectations, and designing an environment of safety and caring. Of course, *you* are then obliged to live by those rules and model respectful communications. Also, easier said than done, but so very important.

You may have to break this meeting into smaller segments

of time depending upon the age of your students. With younger children, I talk about respect and love. The "love" word makes older kids a little uncomfortable so "respect" will do nicely.

Elaborating on the "we are a family" concept, I talk about expectations outside of the classroom, particularly in the lunchroom and on the playground, places where the children are typically without your guidance.

We will be responsible for caring for one another just like a family. If you see someone from our class being left out or alone outside, invite them to join you. We will be friends to one another so that no one ever feels lonely or excluded.

Reflection: What points will I emphasize in my discussion with children on day one?

AND THEY'LL TEST YOU

This all sounds great, but someone is going to put you to the test quite quickly while everyone else watches carefully. Did she really mean that? Will she actually respect us... no matter what? Someone will test you, probably on day one. They will make a rude and disrespectful remark, causing everyone else in the class to freeze. Now's your chance to put your money where your mouth is. Believe it or not, this little blister has just done you and incredible favor. Take a deep breath, put a smile on your face, and say,

Oh wow, that wasn't respectful at all. But that's okay. We're learning together. This respect thing takes some

practice...doesn't it? Can you say that again and do it in a respectful way? Beautiful! I knew you could do it.

Or, as the case may be,

Woops, that wasn't very respectful either. I'll tell you what, you stay inside with me for just a few minutes when everyone else leaves for recess, and I'll help you practice speaking respectfully. I just know you can do it!

Without an audience, most kids are quite capable of reframing their earlier remark in a very respectful way. You beam with pride, tell them you knew they could do it, and assure them that you would love to keep them in from recess in the future for more practice sessions if needed. Don't keep them for more than a couple of minutes. Denying recess to a child breeds resentment and is counterproductive. This child needs to blow off steam and so do you. Both of you need a break. Besides, you want the child to feel as if you care about her and have all the faith in the world that you can help her learn to behave appropriately.

Which brings me to another inappropriate teacher response to bad behavior besides not allowing a child recess. Sending a student to the principal's office should be reserved for the most egregious behaviors. Do you really want to signal to the principal that you can't manage your classroom? And more importantly, do you really want to banish a child from the caring community you promised?

THE 95 PERCENT RULE

These strategies will work beautifully with about 95 percent of your students. A few of your kids have severe issues that require an interdisciplinary approach. Special education teachers, principals, school psychologists, etc. have training in helping children who need more than a regular classroom teacher is able to provide. Use them. Still, that child must know that you are in their corner, their improved self-control and respectful behavior is important to you, and you have great faith that they will continue to improve. You never withhold your unconditional love and you never signal to the child that he cannot learn and improve, either academically or behaviorally. You work closely with other team members, including parents, in understanding and celebrating the child's successes.

CLASSROOM MANAGEMENT EVERYDAY

Just as you teach and review math concepts each day, you teach and review behavior lessons. You praise and reward, you celebrate kindness and respect, you point out concrete examples each day. "Wow, Jason. You were respectful even though you were frustrated. Tell the class what you said to Sara when she accidentally spilled water on your art project. That was a great example of being respectful even when it's difficult."

Sometimes it's fun and helpful to have children play-act respectful and non-respectful responses in various situations. This usually ends up with children laughing and hooting delightedly at the bad examples...but the point is made and will be memorable.

LOVE AND HIGH EXPECTATIONS

There are two things that must be present in your classroom every day starting with day one: Respect (or love, if you prefer that term) and high expectations.

I was giving a seminar once upon a time to teachers from poverty area schools and showing them, via national data, how important it is to have high expectations along with caring if children were to succeed in school. The revolt built up slowly...I should have seen it coming... and then erupted in an angry backlash.

These children come to school hungry. They can't learn. They need to be fed and loved and given a safe haven for six hours each day.

While I can agree with the sentiment, I don't agree this means we must abandon high expectations.

And another startling pronouncement:

I don't care if these kids learn anything in my classroom as long as they know I love them!

Seriously? You *better* care that they learn something!

The finest way to show your love is to teach children. They cannot and will not become successful if they can't read. Your love is the impetus for setting high standards and continuing to elevate the bar to help these children learn. Your job is to teach. Granted, no child can learn if he is hungry or frightened but caring for children's safety and physical needs does not preclude helping them meet learning and behavioral goals. Giving children a pass on learning or appropriate behavior because they are poor, or for any other reason, is not caring. It is educational malpractice. No excuses.

In the excuse world, I also hear about how a teacher can't be expected to undo what's happening at home. My response: You have them for approximately six hours a day. I don't care what's happening at home (unless it is abuse or neglect, in which case you will report it to the proper authorities). Teach them. If their behavior is blocking their learning, you teach behavior along with the curriculum, which you should be doing anyway…but you teach.

THE IMPORTANCE OF PROCEDURES

For you to be happy, and for your students to be happy as well, procedures must be in place in your classroom. The first two weeks of school are critical to teaching and practicing your expectations for a smooth-running school day. Children will be more secure, and you will save yourself the headache that inevitably comes from endless questions like:

- *I'm done. What do I do now?*
- *I don't get this assignment. I need help.*
- *Where should I put my homework?*
- *Can I sharpen my pencil?*
- *Can I go to the bathroom?*
- *What are we supposed to be doing?*
- *Can I work with a buddy?*
- *Can I pass out the papers?*

- *I was absent yesterday. Did I miss anything?* (Nah, we just sat here all day waiting for you.)
- *Etc., etc., etc.*

Procedures answer all those questions, once and for all, without your saying a word.

Long ago, when I was substitute teaching, I learned a great deal about procedures from teachers I never met. Their classrooms and their students ran like clockwork, with or without their regular teachers. I have no desire to talk about some other classrooms I worked in where no lesson plans were in sight, and the kids seemed completely confused about how the day should proceed.

Anyway, in one memorable fifth-grade classroom, a weekly job chart was posted, and children took pride in performing their assigned tasks with care. As each child entered the classroom, they deposited their homework in the bin set aside for that purpose…math in the math bin, etc… and immediately took out their library books and began to read until the bell rang. And the fun began. With the bell signal, everyone stood, the "Leader of the Pledge" came to the front of the room, flipped a switch to turn on a fan strategically placed to blow on the American flag, which began to furl in the air current while the class recited the Pledge of Allegiance. The "Leader of the Pledge" returned to her seat and the "Piano Person" hit a key on the piano and the children sang the National Anthem. The "Math Leader" announced a page number and everyone opened their math books and sat ready for the teacher to step in. Which was a really good thing since I hadn't done a thing or said a word up to that point and was beginning to wonder if I needed to be there at all. Granted this process was a bit extreme, but so much fun to witness. These children ran their own classroom with pride and gusto.

The point is you do not want to reinvent the wheel every day. Your children should know how to proceed with everyday tasks without having to constantly ask you. So what exactly is a procedure?

A procedure is a well-defined process, discussed and rehearsed until it is second nature. Every procedure should be printed and posted in the classroom in the area where it will be used. When a child forgets and asks about something that is a procedure, you can simply point, with a smile on your face, to the appropriate procedure chart for them. (Of course, you can always say with a heavy sigh and a disgusted tone, "How often do I have to tell you that??" But please don't.)

Introduce one procedure at a time. For very young children, your procedure charts may have to be made with pictures or photographs rather than words alone. Take the necessary time to discuss how that particular procedure will be helpful to the class and then practice, practice, practice. For reinforcement purposes, regularly call attention to children who are following procedures. The little stars who like rules and pride themselves on following them to the letter will be in their glory. Others will need a little more practice, positive reinforcement, and celebrations of success.

When demonstrating a procedure, I love to select one of my behaviorally challenged darlings to demonstrate, first the wrong way, and then the correct way to do it.

Alright, children, we've learned the steps for coming to the rug for story time. Let's review the three steps posted on our chart.

1. PUSH your chair in so no one trips on it.

2. WALK to the rug with lips sealed and hands to yourself.

3. SIT on your assigned square.

Mary, show us how a child from another second grade, who doesn't follow procedures, might act when coming to story time.

Of course, Mary, a natural ham, will shove her chair, knock it over and run to the rug smacking everyone she passes. Kids find that hugely funny.

Yup. That's exactly how some kids might do that. Thanks, Mary. Now can you show us how we do it in this room?

Mary will become the little angel of your dreams, with all eyes upon her. She's the center of attention for doing something correctly. Possibly a whole new experience for her.

Wow! That was perfect. Did everybody see how Mary did that? Let's all practice that and see if you can do it exactly the way Mary did.

Don't be afraid to have children repeat the procedure until everyone does it correctly. After the second or third time, peer pressure kicks in on anyone who doesn't quite get it.

But doesn't this all take a lot of time? Yes. Next question. It takes a huge amount of time, every second of which is well spent. In the long run you will save hours of time that would have been devoted to nagging, reminding, explaining, and being frustrated and angry. Additionally, and perhaps the greatest benefit of all is that you are teaching children to be in charge of themselves. Self-discipline and the ability to self-regulate behavior is a skill that cannot be measured in the benefits it reaps, not just in your classroom, but throughout a lifetime.

What procedures would be helpful in your classroom? What procedures do you feel are important? Here are a few suggestions you might think about to get you started:

- *What do you want children to do immediately upon entering the classroom?*
- *When is pencil sharpening permitted? (Nothing is more annoying than being in the middle of direct instruction with children wandering around the classroom. These, of course are the same kids who will need individual instruction later.)*
- *What behavioral expectations do you have for the hallway?*
- *Where should finished assignments be placed?*
- *What should a child do when he or she is finished with an assignment?*

> *Reflection: What procedures would I
> like to set up in your classroom?*

SAY WHAT YOU MEAN AND
MEAN WHAT YOU SAY

Recently I was having a meal in a family-style restaurant and shamelessly eavesdropping on the family in the next booth. When their meals came, the dad announced to their little boy, who might have been six or seven, "Now, remember, no dessert unless you eat every bite of your dinner." And then the conversation went something like this:

CHILD: *These peas are disgusting. I can't eat them.*

DAD: *Well, take one bite of peas, and eat everything else on your plate or no dessert.*

CHILD: *I can't take one bite.*

DAD: *Well, just eat everything else on your plate or no dessert.*

CHILD: *This isn't good spaghetti. Mommy doesn't make it like this. I see an onion.*

DAD: *Eat around the onions.*

CHILD: *I'm not hungry.*

DAD: *That's fine. No dessert.*

CHILD: *I want dessert. You said I could have dessert.*

DAD: *IF you ate everything,*

CHILD: *I can't.*

DAD: *Take one bite of everything and you can have dessert.*

CHILD: *No way. I'll throw up.*

DAD: *Well, you have to eat something. What do you want for dessert?*

Teachers sometimes operate by this very same principle. The kids wear us down and we backtrack on our initial demand. If children know you don't really mean something and that there's a chance you won't follow through on a request or a rule, they will outlast you and wear you down every time.

My own teenagers were familiar with this principle.

JENNY: *Hey, Mom, can I spend the night at Margo's?*

ME: *No. It's a school night. You know the rule.*

JENNY: *Yeah, but we're going to study for the math test tomorrow.*

ME: *No staying overnight on school night.*

JENNY: *Well, I'm only asking for just this once. Lisa's coming too and she's the only one that understands this stuff. Please.*

ME: *Sorry. No.*

My teenager continues to whine and wheedle until I can't stand it anymore and finally say.

ME: *Fine. Go. Just don't blame me if you're up half the night and don't do well on the test.*

JENNY: *Thanks, Mom. You're the best.*

But of course, I'm not the best. I have just given in to something that I know is not in the best interest of my teenager. And I have taught her that whining and arguing pay off.

MEAN WHAT YOU SAY WITH CLASSROOM RULES

Make your rules carefully. They should be few but important and firm. Otherwise, you are teaching children to whine and pester because they know that eventually you will give in. Rules must be meaningful and important. If they are, be firm. If they're not, don't call them rules.

LESS IS MORE

I've always loved the notion that:

One goal is a goal,
Two goals are half a goal,
Three goals are no goal at all.

While that may be a bit extreme, the point, of course, of this little ditty is that we need to identify and focus on what really matters instead of spreading ourselves so thin that we can't accomplish anything meaningful.

The same applies to classroom rules. Too many rules mean that no one remembers them all or puts much stock in any of them. Your rules must matter. They must be truly important, both to you and to the children. If you design your classroom rules in conjunction with the students, even the youngest of them will understand their importance and be far more committed to living them.

You will need to set aside enough time for this endeavor and set the tone by emphasizing the gravity of designing rules if you expect children to be truly engaged in the process. Let them know that rules are not about pencil sharpening or pushing in chairs. Those are procedures. Rules are about big, meaningful, wildly important things, based on principles of respect, that will lay the groundwork for the happiness and success of all the children.

Encourage an inclusive and broad conversation about what rules would truly enhance their classroom community. As the children share stories about what matters is getting along and being accepted in a classroom, their discussions will lead to meaningful rules that everyone can agree upon, invest in, and care about.

The topic of bullying will come up. Let the children discuss it and other themes they identify as important. Don't rush their thinking. Encourage each child to contribute with questions like "Has that ever happened to you?" "What makes you happy at school?" "What makes you sad?" Chart their responses and thoughts, and from those ideas, your rules will emerge.

"No bullying" can be a rule. That's meaningful and critically important...isn't it?

It's fine to suggest ideas of your own for the children to discuss. This may take more than one session to accomplish. That's okay. It's an important process that can't be rushed. Three to five rules are probably what you'll need. Certainly no more.

Eventually you may want to spend a session turning the rules into positive rather than negative statements. For example, "No bullying" becomes "We treat one another with respect," "We speak and act kindly to one another," or "We are friends to one another." When everyone agrees and commits to the rules, they are posted for all to see and live by.

Reflection: What do you envision as important topics that should be covered in your classroom rules?

WHEN RULES ARE BROKEN

You will also want to have a class discussion about what should happen if a rule is violated. The younger the children, the more likely they are to subscribe to the "Hang them up by their toes" theory. What a great time to reinforce the notion that we are all learners, we all sometimes make mistakes, and the "Do unto others as you would have them do unto you" philosophy. Rules must have consequences if violated, of course, but the consequences can be teaching moments administered with compassion and an expectation for improvement.

No two classes will ever be the same, so this process and your rules will be different every year. Listening to and valuing the input of your children is a wonderful way to get to know their needs, concerns, and values. This is a far different process than your posting rules YOU design and then applying the three-strikes-you're-out scenario. It's one more opportunity to truly respect, value, and teach the whole child.

Deciding upon worthy, important rules is not the end. Children must be taught how to live those rules. Using bullying as an example... My second-grade granddaughter, Sophie, knows that bullying is wrong so she indignantly let her mom know that she was being bullied at school. The perpetrator was a little boy named George. When mom questioned Sophie for a description of specific ways George was bullying her, she announced that sometimes George followed her on the playground and watched her. That was it. That's another reason why it's important to include children in the discussion of rules, listen to their concerns, and assess their knowledge of vocabulary as well as concepts. If you have a rule that refers to bullying, you need to be sure that children understand what bullying looks and feels like.

The next step is to help them with a plan for action when they encounter a violation. In other words, you are teaching children important life lessons about how to handle difficult situations themselves as much as possible and you teach them when to involve an adult. One proven strategy to teach children how to respond to any incident of bullying, is termed **Stop/Walk/Talk**. Each of the words is accompanied by an action.

The action for **Stop** might be crossed arms or hand outstretched in a stop signal. You allow children to decide upon a signal they would be comfortable using. When a child encounters bullying, whether directed at himself or another, he immediately employs the "Stop" signal. Part of the lesson is the notion of co-responsibility that goes a long way in helping children develop a sense of empathy and responsibility to others. If you use the stop signal and the disrespectful behavior continues, you then **Walk** away from the perpetrator and encourage others to do the same. If you walk away and the bullying behavior continues, it is time to **Talk, in other words**, tell an adult.

Stop/Walk/Talk must be practiced with your students with ample opportunities for them to model and demonstrate the strategy. If you can engage the whole school in this effort it is, of course, even more effective. In any case, the children in your classroom can be taught to use the strategy. Using it teaches them an important, proactive skill while emphasizing their responsibility to one another.

This is also a great place to talk about the difference

between tattling and appropriately reporting to an adult. If the child has tried the first two steps without success, then it is appropriate for them to contact a teacher. The teacher's responsibility when a child reports an infraction is to ask, "Did you say stop? Did you walk away?" If they followed the protocol, reinforce the process by letting them know they've done a great job. If they didn't follow the steps, encourage them to practice and put it to use the next time.

When the teacher follows up with the perpetrator, he relies upon the protocol as well, asking, "Were you asked to stop?" Did the student(s) walk away? What should you have done?" Again, practice with this child until she's able to understand the problem with their behavior and how to correct it.

Helping children develop social and emotional competence is part of our responsibilities as teachers. To punish a child is quick, easy, and usually ineffective unless it is accompanied by teaching and learning to help the child move toward caring and responsible behavior. This is not to say that consequences are not important. They are. But consequences must be judiciously administered to a child who has a clear understanding of what she did wrong and knows how to correct the behavior in the future. Punishment without teaching and learning breeds anger and rebellion.

Teach the rules, teach the vocabulary, and teach and practice a process the children can use to reinforce their commitment to the standards of behavior they have developed for themselves and their classmates.

NO EXCUSES

Helping children learn to take responsibility for their behavior and their work requires some discussion of "excuses." Whether the dog ate their homework, or the devil made them do it, children must become aware of the importance of taking responsibility for both their successes and their shortcomings.

As a principal I frequently found myself as the last resort for frustrated teachers. Children dumped unceremoniously into my office were always agitated and usually felt misunderstood. Rarely did a child admit to bad behavior or take responsibility for it. Instead I would hear, "Well, Johnny was doing it too," or "I only did it once," or "Suzy told me to do it." On the very rare occasion when a child admitted, "Yup. Did it. Shouldn't have. Sorry." I was usually so taken aback that I praised them profusely and sent them back to their classroom with a beaming smile and a hearty handshake... probably not the consequence their teacher had in mind.

It was then I began to notice how few adults...myself included... truly take responsibility for their *own* shortcomings, and teachers are no exception. Have you seen this little rhyme?

Who's to Blame?
The college professor said,
> "Such rawness in a student is a shame.
> Lack of preparation in the high school is to blame."

Said the high school teacher,
> "Good Heavens! That boy's a fool.

The fault, of course, is with the middle school."
The middle school teacher said,
"From such stupidity, may I be spared.
They sent him up so unprepared."
The primary teacher huffed,
"Kindergarten blockheads all.
They call that preparation—why it's worse than none at all."
The kindergarten teacher said,
"Such lack of training, never did I see.
What kind of woman must that mother be?"
The mother said,
"Poor helpless child. He's not to blame.
His father's people were all the same."
Said the father, at the end of the line,
"I doubt the rascal's even mine."

—Author unknown

THE DIFFICULT CHILD

Sometimes, when you've done everything right, when you've worked so hard with a child that it becomes almost your life's mission and still there is no improvement, you need to acknowledge that you cannot help every child or even reach every child. This is one of the most difficult concepts for good teachers to accept. So what do you do?

First of all, you never quit trying but you may have to accept that a miracle is not likely to occur. Elementary teachers are not trained to deal with the most extreme cases of bad behavior and must seek support. In cases like this, an interdisciplinary approach is called for. If it hasn't happened already, you need to contact the special education team to have testing done. They will contact parents, and all of you will meet together to develop a plan for the child. Special educators, counselors, administrators, and parents together can often help the child make some progress when you alone have not seen results. In the most extreme cases, a different placement for the child may be in her best interests.

Teachers who have been in the profession for a while claim that children are becoming more difficult and that they are seeing more cases of angry, violent, disruptive, and/or disrespectful behavior. I don't know if that is true or not. I do know, however, that one child with extreme behavior issues can wreak havoc in a classroom and make you feel as if you've chosen the wrong profession. Complicating the problem is the realization that you must protect and provide a safe learning environment for the other children in your classroom. Don't try to tackle this alone. Use the experts in your building to create a support team for the child... and for you.

POSITIVE EXPECTATIONS

In life as well as in the classroom, we typically get what we expect. "This is the worst class I've ever had" seems to be a September badge of honor in the faculty room. Of course, it is a bit of an insult to the previous year's teachers of those children, and it's not true. You cannot expect any group of children just beginning on your grade level to measure up to the children at the end of that grade level. That's just common sense. It's also, most likely, a redistribution of children from their classes the previous year, and it take a bit of time for the group to get to know one another, solidify, and become a new group with its own personality and dynamics.

Contrast that negative attitude of September despair with a mindset that is excited about a new group of children just beginning their journey with you on your grade level. Watch what you say. Watch what you think. Realize that each new year brings a group of children less mature than the group you said goodbye to in June and don't jump on the "This is the worst group I've ever had" bandwagon. Additionally, don't let a previous teacher influence how you perceive a particular student. Don't listen to the other favorite September conversation among some teachers, "You Have HIM? Well good luck!"

If his previous teachers found him annoying or problematic in some other way, imagine how lucky that child is now to have you for a teacher…someone who works hard to see the best in every child and refuses to be influenced by naysayers. Having positive and high expectations for your students is critical to their success and your happiness. And almost always most of the children will live up to your beliefs about them. "You are the BEST class I've ever had" will instill a pride in your students and help them want to live up to your vision of them.

This is not to trivialize the difficulty that some children present. You can plan on having a child or two each year that require extreme care and wisdom and test your professional abilities. I suggest that you begin to develop a professional library of your own devoted to this topic, since you will need to continually upgrade your skills in dealing with difficult children, for the child's sake and for your own sanity.

Here are a few that I would highly recommend:

- Korb, R. (2010). Motivating defiant and disruptive students to learn (2012). Corwin.
- MacKenzie, R. J. (2013). Setting limits with your strong-willed child. Three Rivers Press.
- Smith, D., Fisher, D. & Frey, N. (2015). Better than carrots or sticks: Restorative practices for positive classroom management. ASCD.

Check the references at the end of this chapter for additional book suggestions. Remember that inability to manage children's behavior drives many teachers out of the profession. Don't be one of them. You can do this!

BUILDING RELATIONSHIPS WITH CHILDREN: THE KEY TO CLASSROOM MANAGEMENT

Nothing matters more than building relationships. No amount of discipline, no list of rules, no plethora of procedures can ever take the place of a warm and caring relationship with each child in your classroom. That caring will be reciprocated and allow you and the children to flourish.

At about the point in the year when things are operating smoothly and relationships have been built, the principal will arrive unexpectedly at your door with a brand new student. Make no mistake, adding one more person will inevitably upset the dynamics in your classroom. So how do you prepare for this momentous occasion?

When my two youngest daughters were in elementary school, Kate in the fourth grade and Elaina in second, we had a traumatic upheaval in our family that forced our moving to a new location and, by default, a new school. I saw from a parent's perspective what it feels like to take your children into a strange environment and leave them with new teachers who are strangers to you and to your children.

Both girls, having been through so much trauma already, now faced further disruption in their lives, and they were frightened. I took Kate to her classroom first and the teacher welcomed her warmly and assured me that all would be well. As I walked away, with a lump in my throat, I heard that wonderful teacher announce with excitement to the class the news that they now had a new student in class. She made it sound as if it were the best thing that could have possibly happened to her and to the other children.

Elaina, the second grader, was truly terrified and fighting back tears. She gripped my hand so hard that it hurt, and I was afraid she would refuse to let go. Her new teacher got on her knees to be at eye level with this frightened child and told her that she knew how scary coming to a new school could be because she had done it herself as a little girl. She promised that all would be well, that she would help her find a new friend, and that she would help Elaina adjust to her new classroom. "I'll bet you're missing your old teacher and your friends," she said, "but you're going to love it here, too. It will just take some time. If you like, you can write a letter to your old teacher today and I'll mail it for you. She'll be wondering how you are." Gradually Elaina released my hand and then she looked up at me and said, "I'll be okay, Mom. Don't worry."

I wish all children were greeted this way when they move midyear to a new school. As a principal, I walked with frightened children to their new classrooms on many occasions. Most of the time a wise and wonderful teacher knew just the right words to help the child through this difficult transition. Once, however, a very tired teacher announced in the presence of the child and her parent,

"You've got to be kidding. I don't even have another desk. Why don't you take him to Mrs. Blake's class?" That teacher came to my office at the end of the day to apologize, but the damage had already been done to the child and building a relationship with him or with his parents would be difficult if not impossible.

PLANNING FOR NEW STUDENTS

Know that you will get new students throughout the year. In order to avoid an unfortunate, spontaneous eruption like the one I mentioned, spend some time thinking about what a difficult and pivotal occurrence it is for a child to enter a new school and classroom midyear. It is one of the most challenging occurrences that a child might face. With an ounce of caring and compassion you'll never be tempted to use words that are anything but warm and welcoming.

Like everything else in teaching, organization is required. In this case, a plan of action prior to a child's arrival, needs to be in place.

How will you greet the new child? Words matter. Think about your welcoming words before you need them.

How will you introduce the child to the class?

Where will the child sit? Assign a seat and an enthusiastic friend to escort the child throughout the day.

Care for Yourself as Much as You Care for Your Students

I recently came across this quote from *The Good Teacher* on Facebook so maybe you've seen it too, but it's worth a second look:

- *Every school in America has teachers working for free on a daily basis.*
- *Go by any school parking lot early in the morning, late in the afternoon or even at night or on the weekends, and you will see them. No overtime, no bonuses or promotions on the line—just doing it for their students!*
- *Teachers are using their free time, and often investing their own money, for children's literacy, prosperity, and future.*

It's not just the time we spend as educators that can deplete and demoralize us. It's the complexity of the everyday demands of our work. Classroom management, particularly, can drain our energy and our confidence if we let it. Just when you think you're a pro, you encounter a situation beyond your skill level. Expect that to happen throughout your career. All you can do is all you can do. It's so critical that we not allow teaching to demoralize or consume us or we will have nothing left for ourselves, our students, or anyone else.

Ralph Waldo Emerson wrote these wise words that apply so beautifully to the attitude we as teachers must strive to embrace:

> *Write it on your heart that every day is the best day of the year. He is rich who owns the day, and no one owns the day who allows it to be invaded with fret and anxiety. Finish every day and be done with it. You have done what you could. Some blunders and absurdities, no doubt crept in. Forget them as soon as you can, tomorrow is a new day; begin it well and serenely, with too high a spirit to be cumbered with your old nonsense. This new day is too dear, with its hopes and invitations, to waste a moment on the yesterdays.*

Go home. Let it go. You did all you could today.

REFERENCES

Bambara, L. M., Janney, R., & Snell, M. E. (2015). Behavior support (3rd ed.) Paul H. Brooks Publishing Co.

Bates, J. E. (2001). Adjustment style in childhood as a product of parenting and temperament. In T. D. Wachs & G. A. Kohnstamm (Eds.) Temperament in context (pp. 173-200). Lawrence Erlbaum.

Boynton, M. & Boynton, C. (2005). *The educator's guide to preventing and solving discipline problems.* ASCD.

Cozolino, L. (2014). *Attachment-based teaching.* W.W. Norton & Company.

Emerson, R.W. (2010) *Emerson: Collected poems and translations.* Library of America.

Faber, A. & Mazlish, E. (2012). *How to talk so kids will listen and listen so kids will talk.*
Scribner.

Glasser, H., & Easley, J. (1998). *Transforming the difficult child.* Center for the Difficult Child Publications: Tucson, AZ.

Kohn, A. (1996). *Beyond discipline: From compliance to community.* ASCD.

Korb, R. (2012). *Motivating defiant and disruptive students to learn: Positive classroom management strategies.* Corwin Press.

MacKenzie, R. J. (2013). *Setting limits with your strong-willed child.* Three Rivers Press.

Ross, S., Horner, R., Stiller, B. (2012) *Bully prevention in positive behavior support.* Center on PBIS.

Smith, D., Fisher, D., & Frey, N. (2015). *Better than carrots or sticks: Restorative practices for positive classroom management.* ASCD.

Smith, R., Dearborn, G., & Lambert, M. *Picture this: Visuals and rubrics to teach procedures, save your voice, and love your students.* Conscious Teaching.

Walker, H. M., Ramsey, E., & Gresham, F. M. (2004). *Antisocial behavior in school.* Cenage Learning.

CHAPTER 5

TAKING CHARGE OF YOUR CURRICULUM

For every minute spent planning, an hour is earned.
—BENJAMIN FRANKLIN

Teachers can become discouraged by their inability to efficiently organize the myriad daily responsibilities and demands. Organization is time consuming, but, like developing and teaching procedures, it's time well spent. A well-organized teacher feels less stress and more confidence in his ability to be effective with children. With the curriculum, the classroom, and the schedule organized ahead of time, you can spend your days with far less stress, doing what matters most for your students.

THOSE PESKY STANDARDS

One of the complaints I hear from teachers is their frustration with having to teach to standards. Most states have now employed the Common Core, and yours may be one of them. At the very least, your state or district has designed and published their own standards. Seasoned teachers, accustomed to teaching directly from a textbook, sometimes find the requirement to teach standards to be disconcerting. Granted, it requires planning and organization. (Planning and organization seem to be a common thread, don't they?) New teachers who have always worked with standards seem to take this more in stride. Yet, effective management and organization of standards for the year is a universal concern. How do I make certain that I have taught, and children have learned, everything required in this school year? At the same time, how do I make sure I'm capitalizing on the children's interests as they emerge?

So why do we even need standards? Years ago when I began teaching in Utah where I live now, I walked into my first-grade classroom as a total novice teaching 6 year olds. My previous and limited experience in another state had been teaching language arts to seventh and eighth graders. Now I found myself in a room full of tiny chairs and little tables, with one corner full of art supplies and another corner stacked with reading books from pre-primers through more advanced levels. Those were the only textbooks in sight.

And so I asked my principal what I was supposed to teach in first grade. He was as flummoxed as I was and began to look through the closet in my classroom where he found some dusty old paperback notebooks called curriculum guides. "Look at these," he said. "Maybe this is what you're supposed to teach."

I looked at them. Well, truthfully, I perused them and, since nobody seemed to know or care, I began to plan my lessons around my own personal interests. I had lived in Japan for four years and was enamored with all things Japanese, so for social studies, my first graders learned to make gyoza, learned some basic phrases in Japanese, and learned to sing Japanese songs, but probably never understood their own neighborhood or how to walk around the block.

I taught them to read because I knew that was important in first grade. I taught them to do basic math algorithms because I was pretty sure that was what you did in first grade. I'm afraid I never taught them to think mathematically, nor did I teach them to love good literature. We skipped physical education all together because I'm a bit of a couch potato, and only gave science a passing nod that year.

To my credit I did teach them to love great art because that was another one of my personal interests. I brought in prints from the masters, and we talked about them and looked at them and copied them. We studied the lives of the artists and their particular styles of painting. But looking back, I'm not sure these children could identify a circle, a triangle, or square. I would like to track down those children and apologize. I would like to track down the second-grade teachers who inherited them and apologize.

The fault was not totally mine, however. As a novice teacher with no specific standards in place, I simply taught what I wanted to. I had no clear picture of how the first-grade curriculum should fit into their next years' experiences. I had no idea about my piece of their total elementary education experience. What should these children know and be able to do before they moved to the next grade? How can teachers build on the previous year if they have no idea what was *accomplished* in the previous year?

Even in teaching reading to my first graders I ran into some difficulties because of the multiple philosophes of kindergarten teachers who had these children before they were mine. One kindergarten teacher was a firm believer in *only* play and fun in kindergarten. Those children didn't know the alphabet unless they had learned it at home. Another teacher was a staunch believer in early reading. Her children knew the alphabet and had a huge collection of sight words along with some basic understanding of letter sound correspondence. Because my class consisted of a mix of children from both these kindergartens, I inherited twenty-eight first graders all at different levels in their readiness because there was no agreement of what basics should be learned in kindergarten. In other words, there was no standardization.

BENEFITS TO PARENTS AND CHILDREN

When I talk of standardization, I'm not talking about lock step, one-size-fits-all education. I'm talking about a framework to help a teacher understand what should be included in the year. Common Core and/or state standards provide a coherent logic to education. Standards do not tell you how to teach. They do not preclude your building on children's interests. They do not require that you never deviate from what is included in the standards. They do not eliminate fun. They are simply a set of concepts for a particular grade level.

Of course, a problem can arise when one district has a set of standards and the neighboring district has another set, or one state has a set of standards and another state has a different set. Think about the families who move regularly. Think about military families, for example. Those children can find themselves in a different school every year. The chaos that results from not having a nationalized set of standards is real for many families. "My child learned all this this last year," or "My child has no background for the math you're teaching" are legitimate and common complaints from frustrated parents.

You may not like the Common Core standards, and I'm not telling you to like them. They will certainly be examined and revised where needed, and always with teachers as the experts in any redesign. I'm just asking you to consider the logic of having a framework for first grade, a framework for second grade, etc. so that every teacher understands what needs to be accomplished during the course of that year and so that any child who must move from one area to another is not penalized.

No matter whether you believe that national standards are an advantage, you must, at the very least, be informed about them. Nowhere in education have there been so many myths and misunderstandings so, as a professional educator, be prepared with facts.

MISCONCEPTIONS

Here are a few common myths that you should be able to dispel:

- **Common Core Standards are a complete curriculum.**
  Common Core is not a curriculum but a set of guidelines and goals for what skills and knowledge will help students.

- **States and local districts are no longer able to include local history or concepts that are important to the community.**
  Again, not true. Both states and local school districts are welcome to include other goals, including relevant local history, geography, and culture. Local educators have full autonomy in deciding if and how the standards are to be used.

- **No teachers were involved in designing the standards.**
  That's just not the case. Teachers and standards experts, including many state experts, worked together to design the standards.

- **Standards are not evidence based.**
  Nope. The design of standards relied heavily on best practice research including benchmarks to high-performing nations and states.
  In the language arts standards, the National Assessment of Educational Progress (NAEP) served as a foundation in reading and writing, along with

extensive research on best practices and what students need to know to be successful in colleges and careers.

In mathematics, the standards rely heavily on the International Mathematics and Science Study (TIMSS) that compared students in various countries, many of which were regularly outperforming children in the U.S.

The standards attempt to make mathematics instruction more focused and thoughtful. If you look at the standards, you'll see that there is a heavy reliance upon helping children to think mathematically. They are expected to understand concepts that undergird algorithms rather than simply memorizing them. Perhaps the most visible component of the Common Core standards is an emphasis on understanding. That doesn't mean that children are no longer required to learn multiplication tables, another common myth, or ignore concepts that must be memorized for mathematical fluency. It just means that understanding undergirds memorization.

- **Teachers will have no support in implementing standards.**
  One of the real benefits for teachers in implementation of standards is that ideas and lesson plans from across the nation are being shared. Additionally, most states and districts are supporting teachers with workshops, online lessons, and other implementation strategies.

MORE MISCONCEPTIONS

One common error in logical thinking is the "false dichotomy" where only two choices are presented, and a person believes that they must choose one or the other. There are many yes or no issues in teaching, but the dichotomy test applied to standards just doesn't hold water. The argument goes, "We are being required to teach standards instead of caring about the needs of children." That's just not so. It's not one or the other. Do not give more power to the standards than is reasonable. They are a curriculum guide. Nothing more. They do not hinder you from loving your students, providing emotional support, and helping children to learn the things you think they need or are interested in alongside the standards. If you give standards more power than they deserve you will find yourself teaching to the test, and that is the point where you know you're missing the boat.

Time is such an important resource. No teacher should have to spend time wondering what children should be learning or having to design every single lesson on his own. How you help students learn the standards content is up to you. Kids don't need a dinosaur unit taught every year from kindergarten through middle school, as sometimes happens now, but *somebody* probably needs to teach a dinosaur unit. Standards identify whose responsibility it is and whose it isn't.

Reflection: How familiar am I with the standards? What steps do I need to take to improve my understanding of expectations for my grade level?

MAPPING THE YEAR

"There are just too many standards! I can't teach them all in one year!" is a common battle cry among teachers. They are correct. If you plan on teaching each standard individually, you'll never do it. The trick is to organize standards across subjects in ways that allow you to teach multiple standards simultaneously.

So, with your standards in front of you, you have a clear vision of the requirements of the year ahead, and that may seem insurmountable. To manage this, you begin by organizing and mapping your standards. It's always helpful to map this out visually by writing each standard from each subject area on a separate sticky note and pasting them up, discipline by discipline, on a wall somewhere. The garage is a great place since the

people you live with can ignore your giant wall map more easily than if it's pasted up in the living room. It's wonderful if you can do this at your school, along with the other teachers on your grade level. In any event, you are going to be mapping every subject for the whole year, so know that this is a major step that will ensure your ability to visualize and manage the entire framework of your year.

You are ready now for the step that will bring cohesiveness and sanity to your teaching. Remember that your work must be posted in a place where you can actually see all of the standards simultaneously. You are going to begin to organize your standards around topics that make sense together.

You can begin to move around your sticky notes, from subject to subject, to cluster your standards from all the disciplines so they make sense being taught together. Teaching any subject in isolation is far less effective than integrating subjects where they support one another and make sense, and where children can explore them from various perspectives in more depth.

For example, you can enhance your social studies curriculum by teaching songs and dances from the period you are studying. If you are studying the Civil War, why not use music from that time period? Why not bring in novels about people's experiences during the Civil War? Read books about slavery, the Underground Railroad, brothers fighting brothers, and other ideas that bring the era to life for children. Your social studies text may be replete with names and dates to learn and or memorize. But to bring your social studies standards to life you must cluster them with language arts, music, and art standards. Journals, novels, songs, costumes, gravestone rubbings, and other books, projects, and artifacts from standards in related subject areas will make learning so much more meaningful for your children.

Math and science standards fit together quite logically. If you have a math standard that requires children to learn to create charts and graphs, for instance, why not have them chart weather concepts that are required standards in science? You probably have a language arts standard requiring children to read nonfiction books. You can easily tie that standard to this cluster as well. It's up to you. What standards groupings make sense for you and your children?

Once you begin to think in terms of clustering standards from across the disciplines, you will see how logically they can be combined to truly enhance children's learning. And you will see that "fitting it all in" is quite doable.

When do you find the time to organize standards? Certainly not once the school year has begun. Not only is that too late to give you direction and peace of mind, but, realistically, we both know that you will have no energy after the workday to tackle a major task like this. Curriculum mapping, however you go about it, is terribly time consuming.

You now have the security of knowing that you will be teaching what is expected of you. This kind of organization allows you time to think more deeply about your lessons making them the very best they can be, knowing that you will get to everything.

There are a number of excellent books that go into far more detail about curriculum mapping and curriculum design that you may want to look for. I would suggest beginning with books like:

- *Getting Results with Curriculum Mapping* by Heidi Hayes Jacobs
- *Curriculum Mapping: A Step-by-Step Guide for Creating Curriculum Year Overviews* by Kathy Tuchman Glass

Perhaps your PLC group could read one of these books together, especially is not all of your team members are sold on the idea of curriculum mapping or, on the other hand, if you and your team want to dig in even deeper.

BACK TO YOUR YEAR AT A GLANCE

You've already developed your year-at-a-glance standards outline that proves to you that, yes, Virginia, you CAN accomplish all that you need to in a year's time. Your organizational outline for the year need not be detailed; as a matter of fact it's better if it's not. Every class is different, and you need flexibility to spend a little more time on this concept and a little less on that. The point is you have the standards you are responsible to teach (and, by the way, that children must learn) organized for the year.

MONTHLY AND WEEKLY SCHEDULES

Now take your clustered standards and divide them into a month-by-month calendar allowing you to see your year at a glance and know what needs to be accomplished in any given month.

At the beginning of each month, you can refine your schedule for the month and organize your plans week by week. At the beginning of each week you can further refine the schedule with more detail so that when you walk into your classroom on Monday morning you know what you'll be doing for the week. Instead of organizing by page numbers, as so many teachers do, organize by concepts. Instead of working through a textbook, chapter by chapter, you are working through the concepts provided by the required standards for your grade level. You are not "covering" material, you are teaching concepts.

And anyway, no one textbook will cover all the standards you are teaching, so you will have to pick and choose relevant sections from texts and support that with other books, articles, YouTube videos, and hands-on experiences.

TURNING STANDARDS INTO LESSONS

So now you know which standards you plan to teach that week. How do you go from that broad organizational outline to planning individual lessons? Well, let's take a look.

Here's an example of one major topic in fourth-grade science:

STANDARD

Students will understand that water changes states as it moves through the water cycle.

There are two objectives under this standard, but let's look at the first one:

Objective 1

Describe the relationship between heat energy, evaporation, and condensation of water on Earth.

> **INDICATOR A.** *Identify the relative amount and kind of water found in various locations on Earth (e.g. oceans have most of the water, glaciers, and snowfields contain fresh water).*

> **INDICATOR B.** *Identify the sun as a source of energy that evaporates water from the surface of the earth.*

> **INDICATOR C.** *Compare the processes of evaporation and condensation of water.*

INDICATOR D. *Investigate and record temperature data to show the effects of heat energy on changing the state of water.*

With your standards, objectives, and indicators in front of you, you can begin to identify individual lessons. As you look at each indicator, decide if it can be taught in one lesson. Perhaps two, or, less frequently, three indicators can be combined into a single lesson. Sometimes one indicator may take more than one lesson. This is where you begin to identify what can be accomplished in what time period. It's where your expertise and your knowledge of your students comes into play.

Don't forget to look at the standards from the other subjects you've clustered with this science standard and include them in your planning. For example, you may have already determined that there is a math standard that can be clustered with this. Since you are responsible to teach fourth graders about the use of charts and graphs in math, it could be a perfect match to your science indicator number four that says "Investigate and record temperature data to show the effects of heat energy on changing the state of water."

In any event, as you map out each core standard of the course, along with the objectives and indicators, you have a bird's eye view of what must be accomplished in teaching and learning. As you cluster indicators, and determine the number of lessons required for each concept, you can map out your month in great detail, if you so desire, or at least in as much detail as seems reasonable to you and you find helpful for your effectiveness and your peace of mind. Remember that flexibility is always needed. Even with your wonderful plans, children sometimes need more or less time than what we may have scheduled.

For some of you, this organizational process almost feels like fun. I personally love to organize. I love to organize my shoes, my recipes, the space under my kitchen sink, and my life. My husband, on the other hand, sweats bullets when he is required to put six shirts into three equal stacks. Organization is not his forte. Nonetheless whether you find this organizational process energizing or painful, it must be done. No one wants a doctor, lawyer, or airplane pilot to fly by the seat of her pants. We hope that each of the professionals in our lives has expertise and a plan for carrying out their professional responsibilities. Teachers are no different. You cannot go into your classroom each day thinking only of that day. That day must be part of a cohesive, coherent yearlong plan that shows you that you will be able to accomplish the job you are being paid to accomplish.

ORGANIZING A GREAT LESSON

Now that you have every lesson tied to a standard, you are ready to plan lessons. I sometimes hear teachers talk about a "cute" idea they have for a lesson, something they've seen on Pinterest or watched another teacher do. Your first question as you design a lesson cannot be, "Is this cute?" Or even "Is this fun?" Instead, the real question is always the same: "What do I want my children to know and be able to do as a result of this lesson?" The answer to that question is your lesson objective.

State the objective in as few words as possible so that it is perfectly clear to you and share it with students so that it is perfectly clear to them. Once you have clarified the purpose of your lesson decide how you will evaluate it. What must children do (write, speak, etc.) to prove that they have met the objective? Perhaps the evaluation will be a quiz. It may be a written report, a play, a poster, a recitation, a demonstration, etc. Whatever you decide upon must clearly align with the objective of your lesson.

For example, if you are teaching a health lesson to kindergarten children that requires them to know the steps in handwashing, you might choose to evaluate their mastery by having each child demonstrate hand washing or tell you the steps involved. Notice that each child must have an evaluation of some kind. A kindergarten child who can already read and write might write the steps involved in the handwriting lesson. Not every child needs to be evaluated in the same way, but each individual child must be evaluated. This allows you to reteach those children who still need instruction or practice.

Perhaps you are teaching a fifth-grade social studies lesson on the three branches of government. In this case, you might be able to use the same evaluation for every child. It could be as simple as having them name the three branches of government and write a brief synopsis of the responsibilities of each branch. In many cases you will want to tell children exactly how they will be evaluated. This provides additional clarity for children as well as a sense of understanding the purpose of their lesson and knowing what's expected of them.

Now, some of you are saying, "Uh, okay, that's an objective and an evaluation. Where's the lesson itself? With a clear objective and an appropriate evaluation in place, you now have a basic roadmap for where you're going with your lesson. You are beginning with the end in mind.

GRADUAL RELEASE OF RESPONSIBILITY IN YOUR LESSON

Only then do you design your direct instruction. Will you lecture, read a book, show a video clip, or select some other method to help children acquire the knowledge that is required to meet the lesson objective? In other words, how will you teach? (You already know WHAT you will teach.)

Following your instruction, and using a gradual release of responsibility prototype, you will then work *with* the children to further teach the concepts. Perhaps this is where you have a question and answer session, or you work together as a class to list the various roles of each branch of government on the board. In other words, you and the children are working together as they gather a deeper understanding of the objective of the lesson. This gives you an opportunity to see how well the children understood the direct instruction and to identify and correct any misperceptions while responding to questions.

Then you can assign a task where children work together, with little input from you, for more exploration, information, or enrichment. Children can work in groups to design three posters that represent the branches of government, for example, or write a letter to someone serving in each branch of the state or federal government.

Finally, you assign independent tasks for practice while you observe, discuss, and clarify with individual children. This might serve as your evaluation or you may have a separate evaluation after this step.

To clarify, your lesson looks like this:

- Objective clearly stated and evaluation designed.
- Teacher provides direct instruction.
- *Children and teacher work together* for further clarification or more in-depth exploration.
- *Children work together* in groups.
- *Individuals* complete a task. Evaluate.
- Reteach where necessary.

You are gradually releasing the responsibility for learning to the students. The key is that it is gradual. The biggest offenders to the gradual release of responsibility method are often teachers teaching a math lesson. The frequent (and poor) methodology is sometimes to demonstrate a problem and then, with none of the intermediate learn and practice steps, have children work individually.

One of the best books on this subject that goes into great depth is:

- *Better learning through structured teaching: A framework for the gradual release of responsibility, 2nd edition,* by Fisher and Frey

In working with student teachers, I frequently hear them boast that their lesson went "really well." "How do you know?" I ask. And they will tell me how much fun the kids had or how engaged they seemed to be. While that is commendable, there is only one way to know how successful your lesson has been, and that is by reviewing the evaluations. It's possible for children to have a lot of fun and still not learn a thing. That isn't to say that a well-designed lesson can't be and shouldn't be fun and engaging. In most cases it should be just that. You still must evaluate to know who learned the objective and who didn't.

Well-written lesson plans are critical as is your daily schedule. Knowing what you plan to do and how you will accomplish it keeps you on task and using time well. As you become more experienced, your lesson plans will have less detail and be less time consuming to construct, but you will always want to have a clear idea in your mind of each of the steps of an effective lesson plan in a gradual release of responsibility model. Don't start breaking the rules until you've mastered the rules. You need to know and understand the standards you're responsible for over the course of the year. You need to know how to organize cross discipline standards to cluster them in ways that make sense and enrich your lessons. You need to know how to plan good lessons and how to determine how well children have learned. All of this is foundational and needs to be deeply embedded in the way you approach your work if you are to be effective and have a sense that you are accomplishing all that you hope to accomplish.

THE BIG DISCLAIMER

That being said...There is no substitute for children's curiosity and interests. Don't become so rigid that you are not in tune with what matters to children. A great teacher piques children's curiosity and love of learning with carefully thought out lessons, activities, and projects and is still flexible enough to sometimes follow the children's lead. Sometimes children will arrive at school with important questions, ideas, and needs that need to take precedence over your carefully mapped plans for the day. During the first snowstorm of the year, little people need to watch the snow, read about snow, research their own questions, draw, sing, learn poems, and explore to their hearts content.

When a child loses a beloved grandparent, it's important to take the time for books, conversation, sharing, or even shedding tears. There is no standard for shedding tears. Never let your schedule become more important than your children's needs or interests.

Michael was a child I simply could not interest in much of anything. When he came to school one day with a praying mantis is a bottle, we shelved our first hour schedule and began to research the life of a praying mantis. Michael was soon on fire. Here was something that interested him and, as the proud owner of the insect, he was the center of attention. We used some standards that morning that related to reading nonfiction texts and writing four-sentence paragraphs, all revolving around Michael's interest, which was soon shared enthusiastically by the rest of the class. We drew pictures of the praying mantis and researched and labeled the various body parts. The children were interested in learning to shade their drawings to make them more realistic...an art standard.

The most important thing, however, was the curiosity and excitement of the children as they learned about something that was of peak interest to them that day. In our class, we have a one-day rule about creatures that requires us to go outside and release them at the end of the day. When it was time to say goodbye to our green guest, everyone watched it lumber off and felt grand about all they had learned. This is a perfect example of using children's interests as a springboard to teaching standards.

Standards are guidelines. If you let them rule your classroom, you have missed the point, and you may find yourself and your students frazzled instead of happy and fulfilled.

REFERENCES

Black, P. J., & William, D. (2009). Developing the theory of formative assessment. *Educational Assessment, Evaluation and Accountability, 21*(1), 5-31.

Fisher, D. & Frey, N. (2013). *Better learning through structured teaching: A framework for the gradual release of responsibility (2nded.).* ASCD.

Glass, K. T. (2006). *Curriculum mapping: A step-by-step guide for creating curriculum overviews.* Corwin Press.

Jacobs, H. H. *(2004). Getting Results with Curriculum Mapping.* ASCD.

Jacobs, H. H., & Alcock, M. H. (2017). *Bold moves for schools: How we create remarkable learning environments.* ASCD.

Jacobs, H. H. & Johnson, A. (2009). *The curriculum mapping planner: Templates, tools, and resources for effective professional development.* ASCD.

McLaren, P. (1998). *Life in schools: An introduction to critical pedagogy in the foundation of education* (3rd ed.). Longman.

Wiggins, G., & McTighe, J. (2000). *Understanding by design.* Prentice Hall.

William, D., & Leahy, S. (2015). *Embedding formative assessment.* Learning Sciences International.

CHAPTER SIX

ORGANIZING YOUR SPACE AND TIME

It takes as much energy to wish as to plan.
—ELEANOR ROOSEVELT

Taking time to organize your classroom space and materials is another area that's important to your well-being and that of your children. Peace and serenity can flow from an orderly environment, and, of course, it's far more practical to have a place for everything and everything in its place. No one wants to spend time searching for things when a bit of organization could have saved time and stress. Closely tied to the organization of our physical surroundings is the organization of our time. Time is your biggest resource, and using it well also requires organization if you are to accomplish all you would like.

ORGANIZING YOUR PHYSICAL SPACE

Early in my teaching life I was hired mid-year to replace a teacher who had suddenly quit without a word of explanation... a good way to be sure you'll never be hired again anywhere. I went into my new classroom and was immediately assaulted with piles of uncorrected papers, random books, clutter, old food, and what looked to be nothing more than garbage. Two drawers were stuffed with tiny pieces of construction paper of all colors alongside broken crayons, assorted pencils in need of sharpening, and some very stale Halloween candy. Although I value recycling as much as the next person, I suspect that this was an equivalent of everyone's kitchen junk drawer that never really gets cleaned out. Closets were full of old books... notebooks, textbooks, unreturned library books, and a few Harlequin Romances. I could see no order whatsoever to the way books were simply thrown into available closet space. Had I been looking for library books or reading books or science books, I would have had to take everything out of the closet before I could locate anything at all. I suspect the poor overwhelmed teacher could think of no way to dig herself out of the mountains of clutter she had accumulated and decided it was probably easier to violate her teaching contract and join a witness protection program. The kindly custodian rolled in as many of the largest trash cans he could find and emptied them repeatedly for me until I had worked my way through most of the debris. I honestly thought I might uncover a body somewhere in that pigsty.

Contrast that with the previous owner of a cottage my husband and I just purchased. First, the home was immaculate throughout. But what was most impressive to me was what I found in a kitchen drawer. The previous owners had saved every single warranty for the house and stored them all in an organized three ring binder. I don't know about you, but my warranties are thrown into various cubbies around the house and sometimes, inadvertently, into the trash. If I search hard enough, most of the time I can find what I need. But why not just have one large binder for all of them? And why hadn't I already thought of that?

Anyway, equally impressive to me, the owners had posted a list of responsibilities for their grown children who sometimes availed themselves of the cottage for a weekend. The list was posted in the kitchen and read:

We hope you enjoyed the cottage. Before you leave please be sure to,

1. Empty the trash and put the collection bins out on the street.
2. Wash and dry the sheets you used and replace them on the beds.
3. Wash the towels you used, fold them, and put them in the linen closet.
4. Clean the filter in the dryer.
5. Make sure all dishes are washed and put away.
6. Clean out the fridge and be sure to take all opened foods with you.

7. Vacuum.
8. Turn out all the lights and turn off the water.
9. Turn the thermostat to fifty-five degrees.

If that seems a bit anal retentive to you, I suggest that providing clear instructions for grown children ensures that nothing will be overlooked and that the owners will be happy to have them use the cottage again whenever they liked. It also ensures that whoever walks in for the next visit comes into a clean and inviting space.

GETTING RID OF CLUTTER

Books and television shows about clearing clutter and organizing our homes are all the rage now and for good reason. Our lives are complex, busy, and, well let's face it, cluttered. We all have a different tolerance level for clutter, but almost everyone works, thinks, and lives better when their lives have been decluttered.

I'm heading on a vacation soon and planning what I'll wear for each scheduled event. My closet is jam packed, as my husband frequently points out. As a matter of fact, I have two large closets so that I can store my wardrobe according to seasons. Sounds as if I've taken at least one step toward organization. However, as I tried on various outfits in preparation for my trip, I discovered a couple of interesting facts. First, I don't wear at least a third of the clothes hanging in my closet. Mostly because I don't like them. Others don't fit. Some are out of style, but, who knows, those bell bottoms could reappear on the runway at any moment.

Most discouraging for me is the fact that when I did locate a piece that I liked, that fit well, and was actually stylish, I had nothing to wear with it. That nice skirt had no top that looked good with it. The pants that fit couldn't be paired with shoes that were flattering. How did I manage to accumulate this mismatched, outdated, ridiculous closet full of items that were useless to me? Well, for one thing, I don't like to throw away clothes…obviously. For another, I buy things on sale, excited at the prospect of a bargain even if it doesn't quite fit perfectly or match anything I already own.

These habits of random accumulation happen in our classrooms as well, and before long the accumulation of books, papers, expired coupons, craft items, cutsie ideas, outdated texts, etc. can take over. More is not better. A clean, organized, clutter-free classroom provides an environment for focusing on the task at hand. It also ensures your ability to find what you need to actually *work* on the task at hand.

My home office is the drop off point for me for anything I ever want to work on, look at, pass along, or keep. A desk piled high with unpaid bills, expired coupons, article ideas, playbills, pictures, and half-wrapped gifts is not a conducive work environment. Periodically, I must be brutal in trashing what I know I can locate online or what I know I will never get to despite my good intention. And it can be painful.

I just found a ten-dollar coupon for dinner at our favorite restaurant. Sadly, it had expired three months ago. And don't get me started on my refrigerator. I just found barbeque sauce hidden behind other rarely used condiments in a side shelf with a tiny label that proclaimed, "Best if used by January 2014."

But back to our workspaces. Take a good, hard look at your classroom. Can you find *what* you need *when* you need it? Are there materials that you will never use, books you will never read, supplementary materials you've hung on to forever, ridiculously outdated donations to you from the teacher that just retired, stacks of uncorrected papers? If so, you are creating and surrounding yourself with chaos that is not conducive to peace and happiness. When you walk into your room each morning, you should feel organized and in control, not overwhelmed with clutter and mess that drains your energy before the day has even begun.

HOW TO BEGIN

So how do you go about organizing? Slowly. Don't add more stress to your life by setting unreasonable goals. Start with your desk, one drawer at a time. Do you need seventeen pens, six boxes of paper clips, and a copy of *War and Peace*? Determine what you need and want to keep there and begin the toss out or give away process.

Now what do you want or need on the top of your desk? Take everything off the desktop and give the surface a good polishing. Now organize that space so that it is functional and attractive. Add a plant or a pretty lamp or something that makes your desk feel like a welcoming spot where you actually want to work. Bring a bit of beauty to your space. A bouquet of flowers, an art print that you love, pictures of your family, or anything else that makes you smile will help to reduce stress and bring joy. Make your classroom, beginning with your personal space, a warm and welcoming area. You deserve it.

ORGANIZING CHILDREN'S WORK

One of your taught and practiced procedures should clarify where children should put completed work. I like to have a box that contains a file folder for each child. With all but the very youngest, the files can be alphabetized and numbered so that they are in a regular order that is conducive to student retrieval and, also, to ease in recording assignment grades. Papers are always in order. (Have children learn their assigned number to use with other organizational ideas I'll mention in a bit.) I have children check their folder each morning as they enter the classroom to retrieve corrected work and any other items I have placed in there for them, including handouts for the day or positive notes and messages. If you occasionally put a pencil, a sticker, or some other dollar store gift in a folder, children never forget to check it. Just keep track of who gets a surprise, and make sure that everyone is eventually a recipient. I often include a personal note of some kind, and I've noticed that an occasional note from me almost always means as much to the children as the little prize they occasionally find.

Reflection: What can I do to organize children's work to save time for myself?

Storage Ideas

- Get your containers and bins from a dollar store. You can also buy file folders, index cards, and a multitude of other items to help you store and/or organize.

- Store mini whiteboards along with a dry-erase marker in bags and hang them on removable hooks like Command Strips in your classroom. You might number the bags to correspond to children's file folders so that each student has their own.

- Command Hooks can be used for a multitude of projects and displays so buy them when you find them on sale. For example, you can punch holes in vocabulary cards, organize them on book rings, and hang the stack on a hook. You'll find lots of other uses, too.

- A multi-drawer rolling organizer from Michaels or another craft store, with each drawer a different color, lends itself to organizing paper, art supplies, or anything else you like. They are pricy at about thirty dollars, but, if you wait for a 50 percent off coupon, you'll have additional organizing space that stands alone rather than taking up precious closet space. (But don't be like me and find your coupons after they've expired. Perhaps you can come up with a retrieval system that works for you.)

- Use CD or DVD holders to organize your die cut letters for bulletin boards. And lots of parents may be thrilled to get rid of theirs and donate them to you.

- A plastic name badge tray is something you'll

probably only use for the first week of school but will be a blessing to a substitute teacher. Just be sure to store the tray with your substitute directions.

- An inexpensive accordion file can be a great place to store samples of student work to pull out during parent teacher conferences. Have a section for each child and get into the habit of tucking in an exemplary piece of work now and then.

- You can use shoe organizers for a multitude of supply storage. If you've assigned each student a numbered file folder, use the same numbers in the shoe organizer so that each student has a pocket of his own. One of the best uses for a shoe organizer is for headphones or water bottle storage so that these items aren't shared.

- Supply caddies can be purchased at a dollar store. They are sturdy and can be used over and over for all sorts of purposes. Each table can have a caddy in the center of a table for communal supplies. You can organize math supplies like base ten blocks in supply caddies. Remotes, markers, erasers, and other teacher items can be stored in these and carried around the room.

- Use binder clips to store bulletin board borders or sentence strips. Use one side of the clip to hang these items on a hook. Colored clips can differentiate among materials for different groups.

- Snack containers from a dollar store are perfect for holding crayons and are far sturdier than the original cardboard boxes.

- You'll want separate bins for things that need to be collected, things that need to be returned, things for volunteers to work on, etc. Use your imagination and develop a system that makes sense to you.

- Bookmarks, stickers, and task cards of all kinds can be stored by subject and topic in a four x six video boxes. They come in clear or colored, and the colored ones can be used to differentiate according to your own system.

- Scrapbooking cases from a craft store can be used for books, vocabulary cards, etc. You might want to organize contents by month or by theme. You can use them to store board games or work for fast finishers. Check for coupons before purchasing these or anything else. They always have coupons and sales at Michaels and teacher discounts as well.

- You may like the idea of having a clip board for each child. They can be set up along the bottom of the white board. When a child has finished an assignment, she clips her work to her numbered clipboard. This way you can see immediately who still needs to turn in a project or assignment. This is also a fun way to display children's artwork. They are responsible to display their finished project. You are saved the time it takes to make sure that each child has completed the project and the time it takes to post all the artwork on a bulletin board yourself.

FIRST STEPS IN ORGANIZING YOUR SPACE

The key to organizing your physical space is to think in terms of what items you need to have organized for yourself so that they are immediately retrievable as you need them. Then think of things that children need regularly and how those items might be organized. You want children to be able to access materials on their own rather than disturbing you each time they need an item. You are simplifying your own life, as well as teaching your students to be self-sufficient.

Retrieving and using items in the classroom requires training for your children, not just in how to independently access what they need when they need it, but in how to put away what they use so that items are always neat and orderly. Like any other procedure, it may take some time and effort initially but will save time...and your sanity... in the long run.

Reflection: What are some things I could do to better organize the space in my classroom?

SPENDING TIME ON TIME MANAGEMENT

The number of minutes wasted each day in the typical classroom is startling. Using time wisely can make a huge difference in the quality of student learning and in your own peace of mind. Start by looking at the time wasted in transitions from one activity to the next.

STREAMLINING TRANSITION TIME

Children can learn and take pride in the ability to move quickly into the next task for the day. If you have a reward system of some sort, points toward an activity that the children must earn, a marble jar, whatever, reward them for a transition of one or two minutes. You decide what a reasonable amount of time would be and be explicit about what a completed transition will look like.

> *I want your art projects put away and your math books on your desk and opened to page 58. You have two minutes. And... begin.*

This approach is so much more fun for the children and so much more effective than watching them procrastinate while you lose patience. If you haven't thought about the amount of time that is lost in transitions, think about it now. It will magically add precious minutes to your day.

> *Reflection: How can I make transitions smoother in my classroom?*

THE DAILY SCHEDULE

Posting a daily schedule not only keeps *you* on track but serves as an organizer for the children. For younger children, a picture might help them to read and understand the words on your schedule. You're providing a predictable learning environment for your students by posting the major learning activities of the day. It also helps to have a place to post assignments you give. These strategies help all children but are especially useful for children who struggle with organizational skills and with English language learners who may need visual as well as auditory directions.

Posting a schedule is a wonderful step in demonstrating organization and time management strategies for your students. Note that nowhere in this schedule does it say, "have fun." That's because you don't schedule fun. You live and breathe fun. Fun is intertwined in everything you do in your classroom. Children are naturally filled with happiness and fun unless you beat it out of them. The question is are *you* filled with joy and fun and happiness? If you have chosen to spend your life among young children, joy is a prerequisite to being effective. Joy is a prerequisite to touching their hearts and minds and souls of your students. You must be one in their joy. Again, that doesn't mean we spend our days with an idiotic, artificial grin paste pasted on our faces. What it means is that we have spent the time taking care of ourselves so that when we walk into that classroom, we feel excited to be there and happy at the opportunity we've been given to truly change lives. Our work is a blessing.

Sometimes during the day you look around that classroom and realize that these hardworking, achieving, growing children just need a break. This isn't wasting time; this is using time effectively. Have wonderful music ready. Loud, joyful, clap-your-hands music. When kids hear that music (alright call it a procedure if you like), every child jumps up and begins to march or dance or wiggle or just give their little brains a rest. You don't schedule fun, you live it. One of the greatest gifts we can give our kids is the knowledge that learning itself can be enjoyable, rewarding, and fun. I want to be able to say, "Alright, no math lesson unless you all go out to recess…and I mean it!"

Nothing eliminates stress as effectively as being organized, both in your space and in with your time. Organizing your work life is itself time consuming, but the dividends in your sense of satisfaction and peace are well worth it. Plus, once you have spent the time to organize your classroom in a way that works well for you, it requires only minimal maintenance time.

Occasionally I'll have a teacher who says, "I can't possibly live with such a rigorous schedule! I want freedom and creativity in my classroom! No schedules for me! No rules for me! No procedures for me! I believe in freedom of expression."

I believe in freedom of expression and creativity as well, but I don't believe that a disorganized, chaotic environment promotes true creativity or joy. If you cannot regulate behavior in your class, if your class is always noisy and chaotic, if children are confused about what to do, or if there are no boundaries or rules, there will be no creativity. There will also be no safety or joy. Children will have difficulty learning and they will certainly not learn to respect others or regulate their own behavior.

Teaching children the discipline of organization is one of the great gifts you can give them. The ability to organize thoughts and activities is a huge benefit throughout life. As a college professor, I saw a vast difference in the success of students who had the ability and desire to organize their lives in ways that allowed for ample time to spend on doing quality work for their classes. Frequently those students were also the ones who had jobs and many responsibilities or activities outside of the classroom. I enjoyed talking to them about their organizational skills and asking them how those skills had been developed. Most students had to think about that question because organizing was second nature to them. Given a moment to reflect, however, students inevitably recalled lessons from a parent or a teacher who also modelled organizational skills.

CORRECTING WORK

One of the huge time commitments teachers have is correcting work. Some teachers take work home with them almost every night and spend hours correcting paper after paper. Why? You are a person, too. You would not want your students to go home every night and labor over hours and hours of homework. You know those children need and are entitled to a life outside of the classroom. They have hobbies, activities, friends, and a family who would like to be able to spend some quality time with them. Why are you less entitled? You have hobbies, activities, friends, and family, too.

As much as possible, you should leave your work life at work. To streamline your paper correcting workload, ask yourself how valuable each written assignment really is. Is there a simpler, less time-consuming way to evaluate a child's mastery of a particular concept in lieu of requiring a written response? Spot checking students' work as they do it is the best way to make certain that each child understands and is correctly completing a task. No teacher wants to correct a math worksheet at the end of the day, only to find out that some children have completed every problem on the page incorrectly. By spot checking, you can stop errors before they are reinforced. Glancing at two or three problems, with your answer sheet in hand, tells you that a student understands the concept and you can leave them to practice that concept on their own. If they make an error on one or two problems, it's not the end of the world.

You can spend some one-on-one time with a struggling student until you feel he can work independently. Return after a bit to double check that he's now on target. Whatever you do, don't allow a child to struggle with a concept that she is unsure about. You may need to pull a few kids away from the seatwork and reteach the concept. Then see if they can do a couple of problems independently. Make notes on your clipboard of who is sailing along and who you will want to check on again tomorrow with the possibility of another reteaching session. Collect all the children's work and, without guilt, toss it into the trash. Only after the kids have all gone home for the day, of course. If you've given a homework assignment strictly for needed practice, spot check just a few of a child's answers and be done.

Not every piece of work requires your undivided concentration. Choose those assignments that require scrutiny and feedback with caution. Most of us are our own worst enemies with a compulsion to examine every piece of work from every child in minute detail. It's just not necessary.

A CLASSROOM WEBSITE

A classroom website is a valuable tool to inform and stay in touch with parents. To protect your time, your classroom website should answer the "frequently asked questions" that might otherwise require a phone call from parents. Ask yourself what parents might need to know, and then have a question and answer section on your website.

Reflection: What are the frequently asked questions that I could answer on a classroom website? What other information would I like to include on my classroom website to make it valuable for parents?

You need not reinvent the wheel in designing your website. Many schools have a standard format that they want teachers to use, but if that's not the case in your school, you can find wonderful ideas for website design and organization by looking at what other teachers have included. Your website doesn't need to be fancy, but be sure to update it regularly. Nothing says "I don't care quite" as well as an outdated website.

In addition to a section for frequently asked questions, you might want to include things like:
- Standards that are being learned that month
- Games and activities to support learning at home
- Websites and videos that children might enjoy
- Kudos to a particular student or volunteer (Just be sure that over the course of a few months, everyone is mentioned.)

- Book suggestions
- Community activities that may be of interest

And always…a note of appreciation to parents and guardians for entrusting their children to you.

If your school doesn't regularly publish a newsletter or website, you're also going to want to talk about schoolwide activities, lunch menus, etc. If your school does have a website with this information, simply direct parents there rather than repeating that information on your site.

STRESSING OVER SUBS

Teachers, practically on their deathbeds, are often worried about providing plans for a substitute. With your standards week-at-a-glance schedule sitting on your desk you don't have to stress. If you can provide more details for the sub, great. If not, the beleaguered sub knows what you intended to accomplish, via concepts and objectives, and can work from that.

It's a great idea to have a sub folder, drawer, or box, and don't forget those name tags you've tucked away. This is something that stays in your classroom, and the sub can access if he or she gets stuck. Perhaps it's directions and materials for a project that will provide enrichment for the kids. It should contain your general weekly schedule, so that the sub knows what time the students go to lunch, what day and time they go to the library, PE, or the computer lab. This hopefully stays the same all year and is ready for the sub. Add a book or two that the children would enjoy having read to them and an assignment that relates to it.

Maybe you want to add a Coke or a granola bar in the sub box and a message about which teacher to turn to if the sub needs some help. That sub box will allow you to stay in bed with your strep throat rather than running to the school at six a.m. to run off worksheets or emailing long, convoluted pre-dawn messages to the sub.

Stay in bed. You've got this covered. You're organized. And doesn't that make you happy?

PLANNING FOR FREE WEEKENDS

Set a goal to have your weekends free. Teaching is such demanding work that you absolutely must allow yourself the time and space to regenerate. One of the best young teachers I ever worked with lasted only one year in the profession. She was the first one in the building each day and the last one to leave each evening. Finally, she threw in the towel because she just couldn't maintain that pace. She couldn't differentiate between what was critical and what could slide. Consequently, she was unable to build in time for herself, and her mental and physical health took a nosedive.

If you must, spend some time after school on Fridays to plan and finish any loose ends. It's well worth it so that when you walk away you can clear your mind for the weekend. Before you spend a lot of time correcting papers on Friday, be sure that simply glancing through them won't suffice. Better yet, keep a trash can handy. What hasn't been corrected by Friday afternoon can be filed there. Let your conscience be your guide. My conscience always guided me to the trash can. You want the weekend free from schoolwork and school thoughts, and you want to be able to walk into a clean and organized classroom on Monday morning to start the week fresh.

Time is our biggest resource in the classroom and so much of it can be squandered through mismanagement and disorganization. Conversely time can be added to your day by careful planning. Just be sure to build in time for yourself. You matter too.

REFERENCES

Anderson, M. (2010). *The well-balanced teacher: How to work smarter and stay sane inside the classroom and out.* ASCD.

Christian, B., & Griffiths, T. (2016). *Algorithms to live by: The computer science of human decisions.* Henry Holt and Co.

Kondo, M., & Sonenshein, S. (2020). *Joy at Work*. Little Brown Spark.

Levitin, D. J. (2015). *The organized mind: Thinking straight in the age of information overload.* Turtleback Books.

Unger, M. S. (2011). *Organized teacher, happy classroom: A lesson plan for managing your time, space, and materials.* Betterway Home.

Selk, J., Bartow, T., & Rudy, M. (2015). *Organize tomorrow today: Eight ways to retrain your mind to optimize performance at work and in life.* DeCapo.

CHAPTER SEVEN

ADMINISTRATORS: WHAT GOOD ARE THEY?

Leaders are people who do the right thing.
Managers are people who do things right.
—WARREN BENNIS

Some teachers love to administrator bash. From the superintendent to the school board to their very own principal, nobody escapes their wrath. A local school district recently announced their new compensation package for the upcoming year. The starting salary for new teachers was a huge improvement. Steps and lanes on the salary schedule were all increased by a large percentage, and there would be no increase in the portion the benefits package that teachers paid. The district planned to absorb the increased insurance costs. In other words, most teachers would be receiving a huge raise that would not be offset by having to pay any increased insurance premiums.

As someone who has served on negotiation teams, I recognized the amount of work that had gone into this new compensation package, including lobbying the state legislature for initiatives that could support such a large and well-deserved salary increase. In addition to this package, the school board was setting aside a small amount to pay directly to teachers who were engaged in work that supported, not only their own classrooms, but the entire school. They wanted to compensate teachers who developed and/or implemented innovative, generalizable projects that improved the quality of instruction for themselves *and* others.

Unbelievably, some of the teachers from that district used Facebook to complain that they were being "disrespected" by having the district set aside money to compensate teacher researchers and innovators. That set aside money was not to be used for supplies and materials, but rather as another salary increase for the truly exceptional teacher leaders in schools. One of the reasons I love this idea is that I have seen too many great teachers with leadership potential leave the classroom and join the ranks of administrators because they needed to increase their salaries. If the money set aside for this aspect of compensation had been equally divided among all of the teachers, instead of being apportioned to those who spent additional time on projects to increase excellence for all, it would have been only a few hundred dollars per teacher per year.

The teacher who complained most frequently and viciously about this additional funding had also posted just a few weeks before about what a hard year she had had and how happy she was to see her students go. I suspect she will not be a recipient of any of that pot of money for teacher innovation and research.

This same school district has plans to move forward with a bond to ask taxpayers for a hike in property taxes to be used to further add to the basic compensation package for teachers. I'm afraid if I were a parent reading the complaints from teachers about what is already going to be the highest salary schedule in the state, I would be sorely tempted to vote "No" on a bond election.

Sometimes we are so intent on finding fault with administration, that we become our own worst enemies. (And, by the way, as mentioned earlier, Facebook is not the place to bemoan how difficult your job is, what a terrible year you've had, and/or how happy you will be to see the last of your current class.)

SO WHY DO WE NEED ADMINISTRATORS ANYWAY?

Your school didn't magically appear one day. Someone, yes, an administrator, had to find and purchase land. Some administrator needed to forecast population growth areas where schools might be needed in the future and purchase that land as well. Someone worked with the city to see that curb and gutter, water, electricity, etc. would be provided. Someone planned and designed your school, worked with architects, arranged for contracting bids, and oversaw construction of the building. Someone worked on the interior design and practicality of your building and developed an inventory for classrooms...your desks and books and supplies didn't magically appear.

Someone hires staff, not just teachers, but cooks and librarians, aides, and custodians. Someone buys or leases buses after researching and requesting bids. Someone hires people to drive and maintain busses. Someone sees that walkways are put in and lawns planted. Someone oversees the inevitable boundary changes that must occur when a new school is built. Some administrator must work with the unhappy people who are inconvenienced by a boundary change.

Someone must oversee finances, prepare payrolls, manage new hires and retirees to be sure that they are being efficiently compensated. Your paycheck does not appear magically with social security withheld, and the deductions you have claimed calculated into that check. Someone must be an expert in school law and be certain that no laws are violated, no children excluded, no teachers harassed. Someone must deal with inevitable lawsuits when a law or policy is violated or perceived to be violated.

I have no intention of listing every task performed by an administrator. My purpose in saying this much is to point out how much we sometimes take for granted as teachers. Is ours the most critical job in a school system? Absolutely. But without administrators, our work lives could not happen.

Maligning administrators and painting with a broad-brush

stroke simply influences the public to believe that educators, whatever their role, are unfair or inefficient, or (laughably) overpaid. To destroy the trust of the public in our educational system is not something to be taken lightly. Without the confidence of parents, you and I would be unemployed.

WHAT YOU SHOULD EXPECT
FROM YOUR PRINCIPAL

The administrator who most directly influences you and your students is the school principal. You should have a good idea of what you can reasonably expect from that person. An effective principal:

Promotes a Mission and a Vision

A principal should work in concert with the faculty, staff, and parents to create a vision of what they want their school to be. This is not done in isolation. A healthy school looks like, sounds like, and feels like a place where everyone is valued, respected, and able to learn and grow. That school community should have opportunities to participate in planning for the future. There is a great deal of research on effective elementary schools. Your principal should be familiar with that work in order to help you develop a mission and vision for your school that combines best practices with your school community's dreams and goals, along with strategies and milestones to help your school stay on track toward meeting those goals.

Once a faculty, staff, parents, and principal have clearly identified who they are and who they hope to be, it is the job of the principal to keep that vision in the forefront and make administrative decisions based upon that jointly developed vision.

Is Honest and Trustworthy

No doublespeak allowed. Everyone should hear the same message no matter how difficult it may be. That means the principal doesn't engage in gossip or discuss one teacher with another, nor does he play favorites. You should be able to trust that he will be fair and honest with you. You should be able to trust that conversations will be held in confidence and be able to speak freely about issues or concerns.

Can Deal with Conflict

Conflict resolution is a big part of what principals must be able to do. Whether it's a disagreement between colleagues or a teacher and an irate parent, the principal can't be avoidant. Once upon a time, when I was an assistant principal, I worked with a principal who simply hated and avoided conflict. Well, let's face it, nobody loves it. From her office, she had a clear view of the pathway to the school and could see trouble coming. That principal would disappear in a flash, and I would be left to deal with the angry parent. My guess was, though I could never prove it, was that she fled to a bathroom stall where she sat down and pulled her feet up until her secretary came in and gave her an all clear.

Truly irate parents almost always demand to see the principal before they come to you. I had a parent storm into my office once day with a fantastic story about a fine third- grade teacher. This mom claimed that her child had been tied up with a thick rope and held captive for the day.

I assured the parent that we never tie up our children and that Mrs. Jones was a kind (and normal) person. Since the parent could not be disabused of her wild notion, I offered to bring Mrs. Jones in so we could all talk together. When I went to Mrs. Jones room to get her, chuckling about what the parent had reported, the poor teacher turned pale. "What's wrong, Kathy? Come on down to my office and we can get this straightened out in a heartbeat."

"No, we can't. I DID tie him to his chair. The kid refuses to stay put, so we agreed to tie a little piece of yarn around his waist to remind him not to get out of his seat." Oops.

The teacher, the parent, and I talked about what had happened and agreed that tying him into his chair, even loosely with a piece of yarn, was probably not the best solution, but we ended up chuckling about how difficult it was to get this little guy to sit school at school or at home.

Works Just as Hard as You Do

Just because you don't see everything your principal is doing doesn't mean she isn't doing anything. The principal doesn't see everything you're doing either. The job of a principal, done correctly, is every bit as difficult as the job of a teacher. The buck stops there.

Promotes Collaborative Decision Making

No one elected the principal. He is not king. He or she is a facilitator that should hire the best people and then support them in every way possible. Because teachers are working most closely with children, they need to have a strong voice in the operations of the school. You should expect that your principal values the input of faculty and staff and includes them in decisions that affect them and their students.

At the same time, be aware that there are decisions that only the principal can make. Most often this is because of confidentiality issues that must be adhered to. Firing decisions, for example, are devastating to a faculty. They can cause pain and misunderstanding. The person losing her job will sometimes work hard to turn the faculty against the principal. Just remember that issues of this nature cannot be discussed publicly by the principal. You are only hearing one side of the story.

Expects Individual and Group Accountability

One of the most difficult jobs a principal has is helping each of her teachers be all that they should be. Almost always, that is a positive transaction for teacher and administrator. Be wary, however, of the principal who constantly gives everyone the highest possible scores on evaluations or can find no area that a teacher might want to improve. Everyone loves these principals, of course. But part of the administrator's responsibility is to ensure that every teacher is held accountable for doing a good job with the children. Teacher and principal must be able to discuss openly, honestly, and kindly any area in need of improvement…and who couldn't improve?

I've worked for "pat-you-on-the-back and tell you how perfect you are" principals. One day, however, when I started working at a different school, my new principal came in to watch me teach. At the conclusion, feeling that I had done a pretty darn perfect lesson, I was shocked when he spoke for a few minutes about things that had gone well and then identified an area that needed to be improved. Say what? My principal suggested that I speak too rapidly and forget to summarize periodically for the children. I do? No one had ever mentioned that. Incensed, I brought it up in the faculty room so that my colleagues could all be equally incensed. "Well, you do talk fast," offered one friend. "Kinda like a bullet train," another suggested less tactfully and with a giggle. "You know, I just read an article about the importance of regular summaries for kids, and I've been trying it out. I think it's really helpful," said another. That led us all to a great discussion about summarizing and about the pressures we feel to "cover" material that sometimes leads many of us to speed along with or without the children.

That evaluation process works in two directions, however. A faculty must have the opportunity to evaluate their principal and provide feedback on areas that could be improved. The principal doesn't like evaluations any more than you do, but honest evaluations help us all grow together as we strive for excellence.

Listens to You

You should be able to visit with your principal face to face about your problems or concerns. If you need help with a student or a colleague, you should be able to speak confidentially to your principal and know that he or she will listen carefully and help you resolve the issues. Principals have tight schedules, so they may not always be able to drop what they're doing at a moment's notice, any more than you can do that for a parent who wants to speak with you RIGHT NOW even though you're teaching. The principal, however, should make every effort to get back with you as quickly as possible.

WHAT YOUR PRINCIPAL SHOULD EXPECT FROM YOU

Principals are people too. Gossip and backbiting will almost always get back to them and, obviously, do nothing to improve the culture of your school. If you have an issue or concern about your principal, do the right thing and go directly to her. We've already talked about the difficulty of confrontation and conflict resolution with parents. It's every bit as difficult, if not more so, with your administrator. Nonetheless, it's the ethical way to handle a problem.

If you wait until the problem has festered, it becomes even more difficult to confront the person with kindness and an open mind and heart. Talk regularly with your principal, invite her into your classroom, and develop the kind of working relationship you would want to have with any of your colleagues. That way, when a problem arises, you are far more likely and able to talk about it directly rather than gossiping in the faculty room... a practice that doesn't solve anything and can easily lead to other teachers piling on.

There's a wonderful book entitled *The Courageous Follower* (2009) that I have read many times over in my work life. It reminds me that not only does my administrator have a responsibility to me, but I have a responsibility to her. My responsibility is to remain loyal, to be supportive, and to provide honest feedback as I see it.

Again it must be said that the principal may be bound by certain issues involving confidentiality, and sometimes teachers don't know all the facts. A principal can only share confidential information with you on a need-to-know basis, so you may not always understand what's happening behind the scenes. Not everything is exactly as it appears. With that caveat, however, I would still encourage you to become a teacher that your principal can rely on and trust. Your well-thought-out opinions, particularly as they affect you or your students, can and should be honestly shared. No principal sees and hears everything that's happening in a building. Feedback you give can be extraordinarily helpful in leading to good administrative decisions.

In the unfortunate event that you are working for someone who is not trustworthy or supportive, you might think about moving to a school where the administrator has those qualities. Too often, however, we expect behavior from a leader that we ourselves don't engage in. The principalship is a difficult job, and it means a great deal to have a caring, loyal, honest staff who want to work with you to create a culture of positive and excellence.

Reflection: Are there steps I can take to be a better follower?

YOU TOO COULD BE AN ADMINISTRATOR

If you think you might want to become an administrator someday, it's never too early to work toward that goal. You're on the right track. The best preparation for becoming a great administrator is becoming a great teacher. "Principal" is simply derived from "principal teacher." Become the finest teacher you can be.

When I began my teaching career, I had not thought of becoming an administrator. You may feel the same way, but be careful of what you *don't* wish for. The best administrators spend a good number of years in the classroom truly experiencing the joys and challenges of teaching. They also need time to perfect their own skills and abilities in the classroom. At some point, however, you may find yourself taking on more and more responsibilities beyond your classroom. As I think back, I realize that my principals along the way gave me increased responsibilities in the building that I took on willingly with the idea of making life better for myself, my colleagues, and the students. Each opportunity gave me a broader base in understanding the complexities of leading a school, without my ever giving a bit of thought to someday becoming an administrator.

Good teachers almost always become leaders in their schools. They bring in new ideas that other teachers want to try. They take on projects that improve school life. They work for change when they feel it is necessary. They treat others, including their principal and district level administrators, with courtesy, but are not afraid to respectfully challenge authority if they feel strongly about an issue. The finest teacher leaders are servant leaders. In other words, their motivation is to assist others.

We've all seen the "climbers." They are the opposite of servant leaders because their motivation is to improve only their own position in the school or the district. These folks are easy to recognize. They have upward mobility on their minds and don't mind stepping on your face along the way, speaking ill of others, or saying one thing to one person and a contradictory story to another if they think that's what people want to hear. In other words, they are lacking in ethical leadership. Colleagues almost always see through this and refuse to support these folks in their upward climb.

But back to you. At some point in time you may realize that you can expand your circle of influence by becoming an administrator. Your genuine caring for colleagues, parents, and children and your ongoing reading and learning about your profession may lead you to take on responsibilities beyond your own classroom. There are some steps you'll need to navigate to begin the process.

IF I THINK I MIGHT WANT TO BE AN ADMINISTRATOR SOMEDAY

Make an appointment with your current principal and talk to her honestly about the move you're thinking of making. Ask about her experiences and pathway to becoming a principal. Ask for an honest appraisal of your skills and weaknesses. Ask if there are additional assignments in the school you might help with to get a better idea of what a principal does. You may want to visit with other principals as well. Every school is different, and every principal has a different approach. If you work in a poverty area, visit a principal in a high socioeconomic area. Visit schools outside of your district, if possible, but definitely spend some time with a wide variety of principals. Ask them what they like best about their jobs and what they find most difficult. You really want to know what you're getting into before you go much further.

Now you'll want to go to your state office of education to check out the requirement for an administrative license. This can vary from state to state so it's important to know what the requirements are where you live.

Contact the human resource department of your current district to see what the educational requirements are for principals in your district. I would recommend that again you make an appointment and talk directly with an HR specialist. A face-to-face appointment is so much more informative and helpful than an impersonal phone call or a website check. Besides, it will give you an opportunity to begin meeting some of the district-level folks you may not already know.

Look at the colleges and universities in your area or online that match the requirements for an administrative license or endorsement. You'll want to compare cost, time frame for classes and completion, ease of access, etc. Low tuition is great unless you are required to travel two hours each way to attend a class. Make a list of questions you have and contact the college departments directly with any questions that aren't answered on their website. Be aware that you may need to take a Graduate Record Exam (GRE), Millers Analogy, or other test as part of the admissions process. If there is no geographically convenient college, there are many online colleges you can explore, and you may find that online works better with your schedule anyway.

Once you've chosen an institution, the fun begins! The admissions process is always a bit daunting. In addition to the GRE or other exam you'll be required to take, you'll probably need three letters of recommendation, transcripts from previous colleges, and other items that can vary from university to university. Some, for example, require a writing sample or an evaluation form to be filled out by your current principal.

Make a list of every item required for submission, and be as detailed as possible. Instead of listing "three letters of recommendation" write down the names of the three people you will ask for letters. I suggest you ask one more person than the number you actually need, because your request may not be a priority for someone. Courtesy requires that you contact these folks in person if possible but, at the very least, by phone. An e mail is not sufficient. These folks will be taking time from their own lives to help you so the least you can do is approach them as personally as you can. And one more thing, how about a thank you note to these people once they've written a recommendation for you?

As you list the tasks you'll need to complete for the admission process, you can feel overwhelmed. You don't have to do everything at once. One step at a time! Of course, this presumes that you have checked dates when required exams are offered. Be aware that there may be weeks or months before you can take an exam. Not all of them are offered regularly and some may require you to travel to get to the exam site.

Finally, know that the coursework will probably be interesting for you, but there will be some courses that challenge you. You may love classes in conflict resolution or curriculum design but struggle through school law or school finance… or vice versa. Don't expect this to be a cakewalk. Take into account your current responsibilities, both personally and professionally, before you overcommit to coursework. You may want to take only one course your first semester until you become accustomed to building study time into your already busy life.

Knowing what a principal does each day goes a long way to helping you respect and support your administration. Whether you become an administrator or not, you should understand what a good administrator *does* and *does not* do.

It's also great if you understand what your principal *can* and *cannot* do. When I was the principal of a large elementary school with great teachers, I hired a new teacher who was convinced that I had the power to give her a raise and didn't believe me when I explained that that was not something a principal had the power to do. When she finally realized that I couldn't arbitrarily increase teachers' salaries, she wanted me to call the superintendent of schools and explain to her that this particular teacher needed a raise. She could hardly believe that 1) I wouldn't do that, and 2) It wouldn't matter if I did. That's not a prerogative of a superintendent either.

If you don't know how raises and benefits are determined in your school district, you might want to find out, and perhaps even be a part of the process.

Being a good principal, or a bad one, for that matter, is not an easy job. One of my principal friends was confronted by an angry teacher who told him, "You're always sitting in your office chatting with somebody while the teachers do all the work." It's hard to explain to an outraged teacher that an important part of your role is negotiating with possible donors, meeting contractors who will improve the building, soothing irate parents, dealing with legal issues, and myriad other tasks that all require "chit chat." The rules of kindness and consideration apply to everyone with whom you come into contact…. even administrators!

Keep in mind that every person in the school plays a critical role. Being an administrator is one more necessary position. No matter what your role in the school, your work matters. If, at some point, you choose to be a principal, that's great. If you choose to work as a teacher throughout your career, that's great, too, and equally important. Where can you personally offer the most important service? What position will make you happy? There are many ways to serve, and every job in an elementary school is critical to student success.

REFERENCES

Alvy, H. (2017). *Fighting for change in your school: How to avoid fads and focus on substance* (1st ed.). ASCD.

Brooks, G. (2019). *Go see the principal.* DaCapo Lifelong Books.

Chaleff, I. (2009). *The courageous follower: Standing up to and for our leaders.* (3rd ed.). Berrett-Koehler Publishers.

Fiarman, S. E, & Elmore, R.F. (2015). *Becoming a school principal: Learning to lead, leading to learn.* Harvard Education Press.

Fullan, M., & Kirtman, L. (2019). *Coherent school leadership: Forging clarity from complexity.* ASCD.

Heifetz, R. A. (2003). *Leadership without easy answers.* Belknap Press.

Montalbano, J. (2017). *I want to be a P.R.I.N.C.I.P.A.L.: Nine steps that will take you from classroom to front office.* Createspace Independent Publishing Platform.

Marquet, L. D. (2020). *Leadership is language: The hidden power of what you say—and what you don't.* Portfolio.

Stanier, B. M. (2016). *The Coaching habit: Say less, ask more, and change the way you lead forever (1st ed.).* Page Two.

CHAPTER 8

LESSONS FROM SUCCESSFUL NEW TEACHERS

We must be willing to get rid of the life we've planned,
so as to have the life that is waiting for us.
—JOSEPH CAMPBELL

The first weeks of a new teacher's life can easily be accompanied by a giant dose of reality shock. Every new teacher has worked hard, studied diligently, practiced frequently, and sacrificed greatly to join the ranks of professional teachers. Most of us began our careers with joy, anticipation, and, yes, a wee bit of trepidation. Yet we knew that this was the career for us and that we would change lives as a result of our knowledge and passion. All of us looked forward to having our own classrooms and meeting our students for the very first time. This is the idealization stage…and it won't last long.

IDEALIZATION TO DISILLUSIONMENT

For many, the enthusiasm and excitement of this idealization stage is short lived. The shock of encountering actual children (rather than our idealized versions), poorly equipped classrooms, overbearing administrators, bored colleagues, or any combination of the above can undermine our joy and lead us to questions about whether or not we've made a good choice in selecting our profession. I can remember wanting to go home and cry after many of my first days and, to be perfectly honest, also trying to think of ways to wiggle out of the contract I had signed. Perhaps it wasn't too late to run for the hills and get a degree in accounting.

No amount of preparation can adequately prepare you for how complex and difficult teaching is. And so, new teachers must be prepared for the very real and inevitable stage of disillusionment. Disillusionment is not limited to teaching, of course. Perhaps you married the world's most wonderful person only to find out in a short time that he can be grouchy and short tempered. That first child you pictured as a curly-haired, perfect cherub finally arrives, and you find that he keeps you up with his piercing and relentless shrieks all night. The pastor you saw as a true beacon of light and a forever mentor, falls from grace, sometimes before your very eyes.

Disappointment happens to us all, and it happens in all

arenas. The more we have idealized a person or a situation, the more we set ourselves up for the fall. We risk becoming disillusioned and disillusioned quickly. Nothing and no one can live up to perfection. Even ourselves. Visualizing ourselves as perfect teachers creating perfect classrooms for perfect children will not hold up to the reality of everyday life. That doesn't mean that we can't and shouldn't have aspirations and lofty goals. It does mean, however, that we need to acknowledge that we are not and never will be perfect at teaching ...or perfect at anything else, for that matter. Nor will the children and adults around us be perfect.

Know that you are not alone in feeling somewhat disheartened or discouraged as you begin your career, or even many years later for that matter, at least now and again. It is part of life's struggle. It is inevitable. It doesn't mean you've made a mistake in your career choice or that you're not a good teacher. It means you've moved from one stage.... idealization of the teaching profession...into the next stage...disillusionment as you see your limitations and the limitations of the system and the people involved with it. Counterintuitive as that may seem, it's a necessary step in the right direction. There are positives that can come from the disillusionment stage of your teaching life.

Perhaps the biggest, potential benefits of this early stage are these:

- You stop idealizing the profession and begin to view it more realistically,
- You realize that you have much more to learn.
- You make your expectations for yourself and your

students more reasonable and attainable.

- You take a deep look at what it actually means to be a teacher.
- You develop far more patience for children, parents, administrators, colleagues. and yourself.

How long does this uncomfortable stage last? Well, like any other life experience, there's simply no telling. It is a nearly universal stage, but a personal one too. Having delivered the bad news to you, I would now like to tell you that I have seen most novices maneuver through this inevitable phase of teacher life quickly and efficiently, usually with the support of a mentor or a caring colleague.

ENCULTURATION

The literature on new teachers is replete with strategies for helping new teachers adjust to their school. You will certainly be faced with a dizzying array of beliefs, practices, social groups, and subcultures, and you will be expected to learn the rules, both obvious and subtle, and, to some degree, fold yourself into the existing school society.

Much is written about the frustration, dissatisfaction, and dropout rates of novice teachers, poorly mentored and unable to relate to the cultures of their assigned schools. My experience with new teachers has shown many of them to be far more savvy and adept at the enculturation process than the literature would have us believe.

Many new teachers had few difficulties "fitting in" and "learning the ropes" and moved quickly through the disillusionment phase. Actually, many quickly felt confident and empowered and began to see themselves as school leaders, effectively navigating the mores of their school community and, beyond that, engaging in strategies that impacted and contributed to the caliber of education in their schools. So how did they do it?

THE ROLE OF A MENTOR

A great mentor can play a huge role in helping you move toward competence and confidence. But, as you have probably guessed, the quality of a mentor can vary greatly. Some mentors envision the beginning and end of their job as simply dropping into your classroom to chitchat for a minute and announce that if you need anything, you can just give them a holler. I can tell you right now that you aren't going to benefit very much from this approach unless you take the reins yourself.

You'll need to use your emotional intelligence when you approach your mentor again. Is he too busy to really give you very much quality time? In other words, he just doesn't want to be bothered? Or is this a person who is loath to insert themselves where they may not be wanted? The last thing you want to do is be a thorn in the side of a busy teacher who believes in their heart that you ought to know your job and shouldn't have to bother them. Do an assessment of your mentor. Are they sincerely willing to help you and, if so, how often and in what ways? Then do an assessment of yourself. What is it that would be most beneficial to you? What are your expectations for your mentor?

If you're lucky, your district or your school will provide you with a trained mentor who understands her responsibilities. You must still be proactive. In any case you should have a clear idea of what you need and are hoping for before you approach your mentor. Here are some ideas to get you started, but you'll want to construct your own agenda.

THINGS TO ASK YOUR MENTOR

Would it be possible to meet regularly? How long should we plan on? You'll want to keep in mind that your mentor has a classroom of his own and be respectful of his time. You are entitled to assistance and support from a mentor, but you are not entitled to be needy. Scheduling a regular meeting will allow both of you to set that time aside rather than having you interrupt him when your mentor needs to be doing other things. Some mentors want to be your friend; others prefer a more formal arrangement. In either case, your meetings are not the place to engage in school gossip or prolonged personal chitchat. You must direct the conversations. Most mentors will be responsive to your questions, but you can't expect them to anticipate your needs. Be prepared for the meetings. Ask meaningful questions about policy, procedures, teaching strategies, professional development opportunities, and anything else that is important to your growth.

Reflection: What questions do I want to ask my mentor?

You'll have a million quick questions that need an immediate answer. Those are best directed to a team member or a next-door neighbor. Teachers are generally helpful with the quick questions that newbies have. Don't expect your principal to sit down with you to answer your day-to-day procedural question. He or she hired you because they assumed you were competent and autonomous…and they're busy with other things.

In the event no mentor has been assigned to you, you can always find one on your own. A teacher on your own grade level is ideal, but not always possible. You can select a great teacher who is someone with whom you feel comfortable. Approach them with a sincere, "You seem to be such a great teacher, and I need a mentor. I know I could learn so much from you if you have the time." Then let the prospective mentor know exactly what you have in mind and what her time commitment would be. Most teachers would be flattered, but don't get discouraged or take it personally if the answer is no. Ask another great teacher.

It's easy to feel overwhelmed with feelings of confusion and frustration. Ask questions. Be grateful for responses. Make friends. Go out of your way to thank those who help you. Very soon you will be managing the day-to-day operations without a second thought.

GIVE YOURSELF CREDIT

The formal or informal mentoring provided by seasoned teachers can be a powerful tool in your growth and development, but don't be too quick to surrender to the prevailing culture. Listen and learn from senior teachers. But a word of caution. Don't abandon what you've learned in your teacher preparation programs in favor of the practices of seasoned colleagues, if those practices run counter to what you know to be best practices. Sometimes, the novice teacher accepts a passive role and emulates what already exists in the school rather than bringing her own values and strengths to the table. You are not an empty vessel to be filled. You bring great value along with you. No one wants a "know it all" new teacher, so be gracious and open to what you can learn from your more experienced mentors. Just don't forget that you have much to offer as well.

DON'T JUST BLEND IN

Many newbies have the desire and ability to positively impact some practices of their more experienced colleagues and improve their schools. It's happening everywhere. Who are these new teachers? What characteristics do they share? How do they develop confidence and become leaders in their schools?

Once upon a time, my university colleagues and I hoped to find new ways to support our graduates as they began their fledgling careers, and we settled on organizing monthly support meetings. We assumed that teachers in their first few years might be working in survival mode, struggling to simply manage day-to-day processes, penetrate school cultures, and sync their own belief systems with that of their colleagues. None of us anticipated that many of our graduates had quickly enculturated, were working far beyond survival mode and, in many ways, personally thriving while actively impacting the culture of their schools. Instead of searching for ways to provide support we began to listen to their success stories. We stopped looking at new teachers as vessels to be filled and instead began to ask what we might learn from them about new teachers becoming valued and valuable faculty members. Were there common characteristics among these happy and successful novice teachers?

In our monthly "support" meetings we began to ask open-ended questions of our recent graduates, and we learned to relinquish the direction conversations took to the participants. They knew where they wanted to improve. They also knew how to help one another. They took over the meetings and made powerful suggestions. They shared some practices they were using that were making a significant difference with their students. And they discussed strategies that helped them develop the confidence in their abilities that allowed them to be contributing members of their school faculties.

It wasn't long before we *could* see commonalities among these happy and successful new teachers. These novices, who had quickly moved past the disillusionment and enculturation phases, shared three common characteristics that you can emulate to move forward in your professional development in ways you will find satisfying and fulfilling.

COMPETENCE

The first characteristic they shared was competence. This may sound a bit confusing. Become competent by being competent? But it makes sense when you realize that a sense of competence comes from mastery experiences. These teachers *sought out* opportunities to demonstrate competence.

There are many things you do well and probably things you do better than many other teachers. Celebrate each success. At the end of each day, focus on the successes, even if they were few and far between. You *will* have successes every day. Katie remembered her pencil. Freddie didn't cry. YOU didn't cry. These are all successes, and if you acknowledge them, even to yourself, they will grow your confidence in your own ability to do the things you envisioned when you decided to become a teacher. You will begin to see your own competence.

Too many new teachers never realize how important the small successes are. Ironically, what may be a small success to you may be something that turns the tide for one of your students. The timid child asks a question. That may have been a huge milestone in her life and something you barely noticed at the time. Keep a journal handy and jot down every single success that happens during your day, and watch yourself develop a sense of competence.

The most confident of the new teachers not only believed that they were well prepared to teach, but they identified experiences and evidence to support their belief. Being able to express their successes with like-minded others was helpful for them. You may or may not have a support group of new teachers, but you can do this for yourself with a success journal or even by taking a few minutes at the end of each day to review your successful experiences.

Don't forget to give yourself credit for the experiences you had even before you were hired. These are part of your competence quotient. Our novices often talked about knowledge they gleaned in their student teaching experiences:

- *My team can't believe that I'm so good at working with upper grade kids, but I've had a ton of experience in my student teaching.*
- *I always got really good scores in student teaching and a lot of help and good advice. Really analyzing my lessons and talking about what went well and what needed to be improved helped me more than anything, and now I feel like I know how to analyze a lesson for myself.*
- *So glad we had so many real life experiences in the (Teacher Education) program. When I got this job I already felt like a good teacher.*

Maybe this reflects your own thinking. Don't underestimate your teacher preparation program and all you learned and experienced there. Remind yourself that you are well prepared to teach …because you are!

The novice teachers in our group identified technology as one of the areas in which they made contributions to their schools. You may find yourself far ahead of veteran colleagues in this area and may have much to contribute to your team and your school.

- *I have been teaching my team how to use Schoolology and Kahoot to incorporate technology into everyday instruction*
- *I have taught several after school classes for advanced learners in younger grades. We have covered topics like photography, engineering, and coding.*

> *Reflection: In what areas do I already feel a sense of competence?*

AUTONOMY

Another frequent theme that emerged from novice teacher conversations was their need for some sense of autonomy both in their classrooms and in how, when and where they took on additional responsibilities. All had a strong desire to be their very best, but also needed control over their development.

People are at their best when they perceive their actions as self-determined. Choice and opportunities for self-direction allow people a greater sense of autonomy. Look for opportunities to be self-directed, to select projects and committees to work on, and to make decisions about your classroom and students. Our novice group found these choices energizing and affirming.

Don't be afraid to negotiate with principals about what additional roles you are willing to take on so that you have a voice in determining how you best use their time and talents.

- *As a brand-new teacher, I need time to get my feet on the ground. I have lots to contribute, but I'm not going to take on a whole lot of extracurricular stuff this year.*

Our graduates mentioned a need for a sense of autonomy in various ways, but often referred to their ability to opt out of programs or practices that they felt were less than ideal,

- *My principal wants me to take a year to get my feet on the ground before she gives me major responsibilities.*

> *I really like that, but I still feel like I'm impacting what happens here by speaking up at faculty meetings and talking a lot to my team about what I do in my class, like word study.*

- *I'm already doing in-service training for the faculty in classroom management, but I said I would only do one training a month. The kids are my first responsibility.*
- *I'm amazed at how much work teachers here do with parents. We have Love and Logic groups and service on PTA boards and other things that would make me nervous if I had to work with a bunch of parents I don't know. I love building relationships with the parents of my kids, though. I call them just to tell them good things [about their child] and some of them volunteer in my class. That made me nervous at first but now I can get so much done with them there and it's really fun to have them.*

Another way they employed their autonomy was through their willingness to suggest new strategies and new approaches. One new teacher suggested to her grade level team that their students might benefit from more information about literacy practices and took the initiative to contact a university faculty member to set up a training for herself and her colleagues.

- *My team loves my new ideas and even when they're not 100% on board, I feel comfortable implementing new ideas in my own class.*

- *One teacher is like "Yeah, we tried that before and it didn't work" but I did it anyway and pretty soon she was in my room asking if I'd help her set it up.*

Other graduates took on leadership roles, large and small, in their school according to their own beliefs about their readiness.

- *I suggested the second-grade team might teach their children the poem "Jabberwocky" as part of a PTA presentation and it was a big hit.*
- *I organized a science night for the school.*
- *I'm a schoolwide trainer in classroom management because my principal noticed that I'm really effective. It's an area I love.*

> *Reflection: Is there an area where I would feel comfortable helping my co-workers or my school?*

RELATEDNESS

Positive interpersonal relationships with students, parents, teachers, and administrators were a source of strength and confidence building in novice teachers. They indicated the need for relationships in order to have a voice in the school community and an impact on others. Many gained confidence from knowing that they were valued and well-liked.

- *I feel like I am a peacemaker on my team.*
- *I have made personal connections with students.*
- *Many parents have sent emails commenting or thanking me for something.*

- *I feel I have brought optimism, positive behaviors, and a smile.*
- *Being part of a cohort in the Education program really helped me to see the value of building relationships. We all got along so well and supported one another through all kinds of things, and now I do that with my co-workers.*
- *I feel like the parents are grateful for how I work with their kids and they like me.*
- *We're kinda like a family here, and I like being a part of it.*
- *My principal is always telling me what an asset I am to the school and I can go in his office just to talk anytime I want to. I used to think I'd be nervous being around a principal, but we really hit it off.*

The novice teachers who felt most empowered seemed to be the ones most adept at building relationships, not only with their students, but with the adults with whom they came into contact. Relationship building had been a frequent topic of discussion in their classwork, where a major focus had been placed, particularly in the classroom management courses, on building relationships with children and with their parents. All the novice teachers who considered themselves to be effective relationship builders with parents had contacted those parents prior to the start of school. Most of them had made phone calls, identifying themselves as a new teacher, excited for the school year and eager to know about the child and the parents' goals for them in the upcoming year.

- *Most of the parents said that no teacher had ever called them before the start of the school year before.*
- *I was a little nervous to make the calls but felt like it helped me to get off on the right foot with parents.*
- *The parents loved that I called them.*
- *A few of the people I talked to didn't have much to say but the majority really wanted to share the ups and downs of their kids' school lives and kinda talked my ear off.*
- *This gave me so much confidence when I met parents face to face at back-to-school night. I felt like I already knew them.*
- *Making calls is something I will definitely do every year.*
- *Some of the other teachers thought I was wasting my time, but I think they see now how helpful it was in establishing relationships with parents that are making my life easier. If there's a problem with a child, I can call the parent and we work together to solve it.*

> *Reflection: Where and with whom do I want to enhance a relationship? How can I go about it?*

Don't assume that because you're new, you have little to contribute to the school community. Rethink the concept of "enculturation" as it is frequently understood. Embedded in that notion is the idea that you must learn and conform to what already exists in the school. Also embedded in the notion is a deficit model that expects novices to have little to bring to the table. Novice teachers can bring fresh ideas, cutting-edge practices, and positive energy if they feel valued, are given a voice, are able to take on responsibilities outside the classroom at their own pace, and have opportunities to build relationships. .

"Fitting in" is not enough and it is not the same as "belonging." To mold yourself into the school society by changing who you are in order to be accepted will not lead you to personal satisfaction or confidence. If "teaching you the ropes," has been the primary concern of your mentor, you may want to move the conversation to strategies to help you in your quest for personal competence, autonomy, and enhanced relationships. Schools that hold high but manageable expectations for their new teachers, focus on their growth and development, expect them to be contributing members of the faculty, realize the importance of relationships, and gradually provide them with opportunities to use their skills and knowledge will see novices quickly grow in confidence and leadership skills.

BEYOND THE EARLY STAGE

Research seems to show that by about their seventh year of teaching, some felt so confident they stopped learning and growing. Now that's a dangerous stage for anyone in any profession, but certainly for teachers. Educational research marches on. Methods improve all the time. Technology evolves. Demographics change. All these things require that we follow the research, explore new ideas, and be willing to learn anew.

You will never know it all. That seems obvious. Yet we have all heard teachers complain about having to take additional coursework or attend professional development activities. We've met teachers who have been doing exactly the same things year after year in their classrooms, with the same outmoded teaching strategies and the same faded bulletin boards. These are the teachers who complain bitterly about a new math or reading program and won't take the time to understand the research that informs the program. These are the teachers who try to undermine every innovation because it interferes with the sameness of their day to day work. Whether it's better for the children or not doesn't seem to matter. The yardstick is whether it's easier for them.

This is not to suggest that every new program or innovation is worthy, but to dismiss ideas out of hand because they interfere with the same lesson plans you've been using forever is small minded and unprofessional. Be a part of the teams that work on exploring new programs. Study the research. Know what to ask about new programs. In other words, be a teacher leader and a professional.

Years ago, when I was assigned to second grade, a level I had never taught, another second grade teacher, a twenty-year veteran, shared her lesson plans with me. She proudly announced that she used the same lesson plans year after year. She had even squirreled away reading books from a long-ago adoption and was using those with her students instead of the current research-based reading program. She wasn't incorporating appropriate technology because it wasn't a part of her twenty-year-old lesson plans. She knew exactly which worksheets she would use each month, copied in advance, because they never varied despite the different needs of her students. Some of those worksheets looked as if they'd come from a one-room schoolhouse in the nineteenth century.

Not only do we have an obligation to stay current with best practices, we have an obligation to help our parents understand why we teach the way we do. Most parents remember teaching methods from their childhood and can't understand anything else unless you anticipate their concerns and help them understand.

Parents most often complain about what is commonly termed "new math." One great teacher I know assigned a math problem to parents on back-to-school night. She asked them to figure out how many handshakes there would be in the classroom if each one of the parents shook hands just once with every other parent. That's a fairly simple problem that she assigned to parent teams to discuss and solve. That's all the information she gave them, and then she turned them loose to work. Now, as you may or may not know, there's a fairly simple formula for solving a problem of that kind. Some parents remembered that there *was* a formula, but no one ever remembered it.. The formula, by the way is,

$$N(n-1)/2$$

Then she talked about the problem of simply memorizing algorithms and calling that learning math. She shared the algorithm, which made little sense to the parents, and then did a demonstration. She had a group of six parents come to the front of the room and actually shake hands and then a group of fifteen parents come up and shake hands. The parents began to see a pattern and could then accurately predict how many handshakes would occur in the room if everyone were to shake hands with everyone else. Suddenly the formula made sense. The teacher was then able to talk about understanding math on a conceptual level and thinking like a mathematician in a way that the parents understood. The issue of "new math" and disgruntled parents was solved just that easily and with a lot of laughter along the way.

GROWING INTO YOUR ROLE

As a new teacher, you can find working with parents, administrators, or even other teachers to be a bit intimidating. That's okay. Your teacher training program did little to prepare you for these interactions because your primary focus is with your students. Know that, like any other skill, interacting with a school community, beyond the children, will become easier with practice. Be patient with yourself as you move through the stages of your professional life. You'll get there and then, of course, there will always be more to master!

REFERENCES

Bressman, S., Winter, J. S., & Efron, S. E. (2018). Next generation mentoring: Supporting teachers beyond induction. *Teaching and Teacher Education*, 73, 162-170.

Bronfenbrenner, U. (1979). *The ecology of human development.* Harvard University Press.

Dasa, L., & Derose, D. S. (2017). Get in the teacher zone: A perception study of preservice teachers and their teacher identity Issues. *Teacher Education 26*(1),101-113.

Mahmood, S. (2013). Reality shock: New early childhood education teachers. *Journal of Early Childhood Teacher Education 34*(2), 154-170.

Schutz, P. A., Hong, J., & Francis, D. C. (2018). *Research on teacher identity: Mapping challenges and innovations.* Springer Publishing.

Watzke, J. L. (2003). Longitudinal study of stages of beginning teacher development in a field-based teacher education program. *The Teacher Educator 38*(3).

Wesley, D. C. (2003). Nurturing the novices. *Phi Delta Kappan, 84*(6), 466-470.

Wong, H. (2004). Induction programs that keep new teachers teaching and improving. *NASSP Bulletin, 8, 88*(638), 41-58.

CHAPTER NINE

PROFESSIONAL DEVELOPMENT THAT MATTERS

Anything worth doing, is worth doing poorly.
—ANONYMOUS

Huh? I love that little saying. It simply means, no matter the endeavor, we all begin as novices. For example, I still don't know how to ski, despite living near some of the best skiing in the world. I'm not willing to stand up and fall down on the bunny slope. I don't want the embarrassment of landing repeatedly on my (as we say in elementary education) "sit-upon." And because I'm not willing to be a novice and do something poorly, I've never learned to ski. But you can't be good at something, until you've been a beginner.

STAYING CURRENT

To keep up with the myriad innovations and new information, we are all novices at some aspect of our jobs. Technology, for instance, is always changing. Keeping up with innovations that can enhance our classroom seems to be a fulltime job some days. What about new strategies for teaching math? Years ago it was all about drill and kill and memorization of formulas. Now we place much more emphasis on understanding concepts first. New knowledge about how the brain works has made a huge impact on how we design lessons. Inclusion of non-English speakers in meaningful ways requires that we understand and use strategies developed for supporting these children. And these are just a few examples. How in the world can we be expected to keep up with the ever changing landscape of education? Two words: Professional Development.

(Some) professional development classes are amazing. Not only do we learn new concepts and ideas, we become motivated and excited to implement them. Other classes… well, not so much. Before you attend a class, check with some folks who have previously attended. Find out if it is worth your time. College classes are often cutting edge but may require out-of-pocket tuition. What about open source classes online? There are more and more universities opening their lectures and courses to viewers around the country. Even YouTube videos can provide new ways of improving your skills. Struggling with how to teach a particular concept in science for example? Someone (or many someones) has posted videos to spark great ideas that you can try.

Again, don't overlook your colleagues as a source of great professional development. Ask for their suggestions and advice. Visit their classrooms to watch them in action. Be willing to admit that you are a novice in some area or another and learn from an expert in your school.

Have your principal subscribe to the best education journals. A current professional library is a must in every school.

SELF-REFLECTION AS A TOOL FOR LEARNING

Your critical analysis of your own teaching is another wonderful source of professional development. You should take a few minutes at the end of each lesson to evaluate the children's understanding and performance on whatever little evaluation you have constructed to check each child's comprehension. An evaluation, remember, can be as simple as a small set of problems, one question, a quick write, or anything else that matches your lesson objective and reveals who learned the concept taught and who didn't. Without that quick but carefully designed evaluation at the conclusion of your lesson, it's easy to miss the child or two (or sometimes more) who missed the point altogether. Group work assigned to deepen children's understanding of the objective is an important learning step but cannot tell you as much as a quick individual response.

Analyzing who learned what also gives you an opportunity to think of ways you might do a better job next time.

Is there a better example you could have provided or a more effective group activity that might have helped every learner to master the concept? If the unexamined life is not worth living, the unexamined lesson is not worth teaching!

ACTION RESEARCH

If you have not heard of or engaged in action research, this is a possibility for professional development that takes you to a deeper level of self-reflection. AR is a professional development you conduct in your own classroom with your own students. No need to rush from work to the district office for a class; no need to pay tuition; no need to add more time to your already packed workday.

Don't let the word "research" scare you. AR basically involves designing a question of your own choosing that you would like to know the answer to and working with your own students to find answers.

Steps for your action research project include:
- *Designing your question*
- *Planning a strategy for answering your question*
- *Collecting data from your class*
- *Analyzing your data*
- *Taking action, ergo the name "action research"*

So what kinds of questions might interest you. If your action research is to be truly meaningful, it is important that the question be authentic. What have you been wondering about? What would you like to know more about? What do you think might help you with your professional practice?

Questions are limitless, of course, with one caveat. You don't want a question that can be answered with a yes or a no. Here are a few questions other teachers have come up with that may stimulate your thinking:

- *How will daily journal writing affect my students' attitudes about writing?*
- *What effect will using math manipulatives have on my students?*
- *How will assigning reading buddies for daily oral practice improve student fluency and comprehension?*
- *What effect will regular personal interviews with my students about their learning have on their motivation?*

Once you've identified your question, you'll want to think about how you might design your project to gather the data (information) you need to answer your question. A first step in that information gathering is to see what the education literature has to say about your question. Finding and reading journal articles about your topic may provide additional knowledge, ideas, and motivation to see how you and your children will compare with other studies that have been done. Reviewing literature may also help you to further refine your question or lead to new questions. Remember that action research is for you and your class.

This model is a suggestion to get you thinking about how you can proceed in improving your practice in the ways that work for you. Sometimes mandatory professional development, required from administrators at the school or district level, just doesn't fit your needs. We know that "one size does not fit all" applies to children; it also applies to teachers. And realistically, you can plan on being completely exhausted when you go home at the end of the day. So where do you find the time and energy for ongoing learning? Maybe it needs to be built into your regular workday.

There is no wrong way to go about studying your own practice. It will be meaningful because it will help you develop in the areas you select for yourself and your children.

PROFESSIONAL LEARNING COMMUNITIES

Many schools use Professional Learning Communities as a source of professional growth and improvement. What is a Professional Learning Community (PLC) and how can it be most effective?

A PLC is a small group of teachers working together on a regular basis to improve their abilities for the sake of their students. In elementary schools, the groups are usually grade-level teams. Sometimes a topic of study has been assigned to them, but more often, the group itself selects a topic for study and improvement and meets on a regular basis.

As a college professor, I have had many opportunities to attend PLCs. My student teachers, always included in these meetings, came back to discuss their experiences, and they were wildly disparate. Some teacher groups spend their time bemoaning the hour as imposed upon them when they could be correcting papers or engaging in other necessary tasks. They saw little or no value in regularly working with their colleagues to identify areas they might improve. These meetings, of course, become self-fulfilling prophesies. They *were* of little value. My elderly Aunt Florence once told me, "I learned everything I need to know in high school." These types of teachers remind me of Aunt Florence.

Other PLCs work diligently and collaboratively on topics of their choice. They examine test scores and identify areas in need of more thought and study to help students. In one such PLC, fourth-grade teachers were dissatisfied with their children's performance in science. The children in one classroom were learning and performing well, but that was not the case in the other three classrooms. So, what was happening in the successful class? Teachers talked about their methods for teaching science and interrogated the teacher who seemed to be having success. She shared some of her ideas and invited her colleagues to come into her classroom to observe a science lesson. The teachers also decided to invite a science methods professor from the local college to join them for one of their meetings to be a part of their discussion and possibly recommend books and articles that might support their efforts for improvement.

In another school I visited, the fifth-grade teachers felt inadequate in their classroom management strategies and identified that as an area they would like to work on and improve. They reviewed an assortment of online books devoted to that subject, selected one, and had their principal order a copy for each of them. They devoted the next few months to reading and discussing, trying out new ideas, and reporting back to one another. They were excited enough about their new expertise that they asked to do a presentation in a faculty meeting to share their learning with other colleagues.

Attitude is everything. Approaching our work life with an eye to becoming the very best teacher we can be almost always leads to respect from colleagues and parents, as well as motivated and successful students. We become valued members of our school community and feel a deeper sense of satisfaction in our work life. No one else can bestow the gift of satisfaction upon you. You must seek it and earn it through an ongoing commitment to self-improvement and excellence. Knowing you are great at your job is the key to satisfaction and happiness in the workplace.

Professional development is not just about taking classes. It's a continuous striving toward excellence knowing that no one ever really attains it. It's not like climbing Mt. Kilimanjaro where you can get to the top and say, "Wahoo, I've done it!" Keep on keepin' on. No matter how long you've been teaching, there is always more to learn…and the more you learn the happier you'll be.

REFERENCES

Deci, E. L. (1975). *Intrinsic motivation*. Putnam.

Duckworth, A. (2016). *Grit: The power of passion and perseverance*. Scribner.

Dweck, C. S. (2008). *Mindset: The new psychology of success*. Random House.

Harter, S. (1978). Effectance motivation reconsidered: Toward a developmental model. *Human Development, 1*, 661-669.

Fullan, M. (2001). *The new meaning of educational change* (3rd ed.). Teachers College Press.

Ritchie, J. S., & Wilson, D. E. (2000). *Teacher narrative as critical inquiry: Rewriting the script*. Teachers College Press.

CHAPTER 10

NOBODY'S PERFECT

The perfect teacher, the perfect curriculum, the perfect lesson do not exist. We are all works in progress.
—LOUISE EL YAAFOURI

Mistakes are part of every day. Every expert in every field began as a novice and cared deeply enough to continue to work and study and practice. That's what good teachers do, as well. You will make mistakes, both big and little, every day for your entire career. I once had an entire parent teacher conference with Brian's parents who were perplexed by my report of his continuing to cry each day in school for the first five minutes or so. They told me how excited he was to come to school, and none of us could figure out his odd behavior once he arrived. It wasn't until a day later that I realized I had been talking to these parents about the wrong Brian! (I had two of them in my class.)

Another time, I was screaming across the room at Leroy, a new first grader who was busily writing a story but couldn't remember how to spell "fun." Engaged with another child I simply hollered to Leroy across the room, "F-U-N."

Leroy replied, "S-U-N?"

"Not S...F!!!" I shouted. And to give him time to write, I continued in my frustrated, shrill voice:

Me: F. FU.

Leroy: SU?

"FU...FU...FU," I screeched. I didn't realize what I was saying until I saw my aghast principal standing in the doorway with a look of total horror on his face. Try to explain that one away.

And now I'm going to tell you my deepest darkest most shameful secret. On my very first day of teaching first grade in a new state in a new district in a new school ...on my very first day mind you... I lost all twenty-six of my children. Lost them. I had never taught first grade. My previous experience had been with junior high students, and I was rightfully nervous about starting the year off right. I had worked on lesson plans for weeks, had organized every aspect of my classroom, had decorated beautifully from ceiling to floor, had borrowed dozens of fascinating library books, had set up learning stations and enrichment corners. I organized a wonderful corner for free reading complete with a bathtub and dozens of throw pillows. I had purchased a hamster. I had traded in my adorable high heels for loafers. I was ready.

Most of the children came in with their parents. A few (children *and* parents) shed a tear or two. Most seemed happy and eager to be first graders. Soon the parents left, and I was alone with my twenty-six new charges. That's when the trouble began. None of them cared about my wonderful lesson plans. Discipline strategies that worked so wonderfully in seventh and eighth grade had no effect on these little people. I put both hands on my hips and gave my finest evil stare to the offending children to no avail. That had always worked with 12 year olds. I encouraged everyone to be seated and to listen, but these children had ideas of their own. What was I to do? Abandon ship? Run for the hills? Was it too late for me to change my mind about teaching little people?

In desperation I decided to take the children to the restrooms to give myself a few minutes for deep breaths and regrouping. Together we marched down the hall where I sent all the girls into the girls' bathroom and all the boys into the boys' bathroom while I stood in the hall doing yoga poses and taking deep breaths. It suddenly came to me. I would march them back to the classroom, gather them close together around me near my rocking chair, and tell them a wonderful story that would capture their attention and give me the opportunity to settle them down. Yes, that's what I would do. My beautiful lesson plans could wait until later or tomorrow or next week. I knew I had to first get control. *Alright, I can manage this. I'll enchant my little darlings with a wonderful book.* I cannot tell you how much better I felt, how much confidence I had, how I congratulated myself on

202 | SANDY WILBURN PETERSEN, PH.D.

my flexibility. I waited a few more minutes for children to return to the hallway…but no one came back out.

Glancing out of the front windows, I noticed dozens of happy children running through the neighborhood. They looked as if they were school age, and I wondered why they weren't enrolled, until I recognized one of them. And then another. In a blind panic, I pushed open the restroom doors and realized that there were exits from the bathrooms that led outside. My class had dismissed themselves and were all merrily heading home. I had to run to the principal's office, admit what had happened, and frantically ask for help. The principal, the school secretary, and I took off running trying to capture twenty-six merry escapees. We collected all but two. You have no idea how upset parents are when you call to tell them you've lost their child. As I said, nobody's perfect…and I didn't get fired.

The beautiful thing about teaching is that every day feels like a fresh start. Thank goodness. Some days the clock doesn't seem to move at all. Some days you wonder if anyone has heard a word you've said. Some days you want to tear your hair out in frustration. Just make it to three o'clock. Tomorrow will be better. It almost always is.

Teachers always seem to be expecting perfection from themselves. Why do we expect perfection in ourselves when we would never expect perfection in our spouses? Well, it would be nice if we could expect perfection there, but we don't. We don't expect our students to be perfect. We don't expect perfection in our world. Yet, we feel bad about ourselves when we make mistakes. Some of us feel bad about ourselves when we make even the tiniest mistake or don't quite reach our goals. Nothing in this world is perfect and, since you are part of the world, neither are you.

Honestly, the children I worry most about are the ones who think they must be perfect every day in everything. These are the children who feel so much pressure. Sometimes the best lesson we can help them learn is that mistakes are OK. Mistakes are steppingstones to learning and growing and improving. You've seen these children and so have I. Perhaps you *were* one of these children, and perfectionist tendencies have followed you through your life. Very often these little ones are highly intelligent and expect more of themselves that is reasonably possible. They have not learned how to deal with even the slightest perceived failure. I see these students in my college classes as well. They are upset beyond reason when they earn a B on a quiz or an A minus as a final grade. The grade, the outward symbol, becomes more important than the actual learning. I once had a very bright college student who had earned a B in my class, follow me around the classroom saying over and over, "But you don't understand…I'm gifted!"

Most of us learn at an early age that there are always others more gifted, more talented, more able than we are in many areas, and we come to accept that. Sometimes we come to celebrate that. How wonderful that there are people in the world who are extraordinarily talented in so many areas. The problem arises when we are so demanding of ourselves that we are constantly comparing ourselves to a standard that is unrealistic. The gifted engineer may not be able to carry a tune. The gifted pianist may have no people skills. We cannot all be amazing at everything. So what?

REFLECT ON WHAT YOU HAVE ACCOMPLISHED

So, you have found a kindred soul or two among the faculty and relate pretty well to your mentor and to your principal. Hurray.

- You are usually organized. Hurray.
- You have good relationships with most of your parents. Hurray.
- Your children understand rules and procedures and, most of the time, most everything goes well. Hurray.

Every day will bring challenges no matter how wonderful you are. It's inevitable. It's why teaching requires well educated professional people, and that's what you are. Teachers need knowledge, skills, and fortitude to cope with the daily challenges. Challenges will disappear, but new ones will arise. Always.

Life is not a competition. Life is for living and enjoying, learning, and growing, and being everything we were intended to be. Being everything we *can* be. When I compare myself to another I do us both a disservice. We can only be who we are, striving always to be our best version while remembering that perfection is unattainable no matter how "gifted" we are or how hard we work.

EXPECT THE UNEXPECTED

One of my former colleagues, Mr. Parker, had a beautifully organized classroom where every child felt loved and empowered. It had taken many weeks, but everyone understood behavioral expectations and standard procedures. He looked forward to coming to work on Monday mornings seeing his fourth-grade class again. They were a harmonious and loving family, except when they weren't. And today they weren't.

Jason walked into the classroom in a foul mood and ready for a fight with the first person who bothered him. When no one did, he took matters into his own hands and gave Trey a shove, knocking his head against the desk and loosening one of his front teeth. Mr. Parker started his Monday morning with a phone call to Trey's parents to tell them that they would need to make an emergency trip to the dentist, requiring one of them to leave work. Then he made a call to Jason's father to let him know what had happened at school and inquire as to whether they knew why their son was so upset and disagreeable this morning.

Neither set of parents was happy with Mr. Parker, and this was not the start of the beautiful week he thought was waiting for him. When teaching children, the only thing you can be 100 percent certain of is that every day will bring new and unanticipated challenges.

As soon as something goes wrong, many of us begin to doubt our abilities and blame ourselves. And that's why we need to understand our limitations. You are not responsible for everything that happens to your students when they are not in your control, and sometimes you can't even be held responsible for things that happen when they *are* in your control.

No one could not have anticipated that Jason, normally a fairly well-behaved child, would give Trey that shove. Children come with their own feelings and emotions and problems. They will not and cannot be expected to perform admirably all day every day. And neither can you.

Jason's dad told him that morning that they would have to put down their 12-year-old lab. Link had been in the family since before Jason was born.

In all likelihood, Trey's tooth will stabilize, parents will forgive and forget, and life will go on. When the dust settles, you can allow Jason to talk about Link, bring pictures of him, and share how he felt when he found out that his beloved pet would be going to doggie heaven. Jason still needs to apologize to Trey, but all of this can happen in good time and be an important life lesson that your class can share.

This is another place where good books, judiciously chosen, can help children to learn coping skills for universal and inevitable losses. *The 10th Good Thing about Barney,* by Judith Viorst, tells the story of a boy who has lost his pet and helps himself ease the pain by thinking of all the good things he wants to remember about his dearly departed cat. Another book that deals with loss, but in this case the loss of a grandparent, is *My Grandson Lew,* by Charlotte Zolotow. No matter how many times I read that sweet book, it brings me to tears. It's about a mother and her child, both quietly missing the beloved grandfather and finally sharing their feelings with one another.

If your students are little older, the classic *Where the Red Fern Grows*, by Wilson Rawls, teaches many life lessons, not the least of which is coping with loss. But, for heaven's sake, read the book; don't show the movie. No two-hour movie can ever approximate the richness of a well-written book nor can it develop a love of literature in your children. Remember to stay abreast of new books by going to the Newberry and Caldecott award winners each year and by checking the National Librarians Association recommendations, but don't forget some of the classics. They're classics for a reason. Your own school librarian might be a great source of recommendations for you.

Expect the unexpected. Have good books on your shelf. Have patience with yourself. And know that your best plans will sometimes have to be put aside to deal with emergencies.

HUMILITY

Acknowledging that there are areas where you could benefit from the knowledge and wisdom of your colleagues requires humility. Asking for help requires humility. Being authentic rather than pretending to know what you don't know or be what you aren't, requires humility.

I have gone into new positions afraid that by asking questions I would look foolish. What I found was, after months and months in a position, people expected me to know answers that I sometimes didn't know because I had foolishly refused to ask questions early on. Your first little while as a teacher is a special period of growth and develop. It is also the perfect time to say, "Could you please help me? I don't know how to …" or "How can I find out…?" or "How would you handle this situation?" All these questions and statements require humility, but remember you're not fooling anyone by pretending to know more than you do.

GRATITUDE

I have long thought that people who are filled with gratitude must be the happiest people in the world. I have seen so many examples of folks, immensely blessed, who are immensely unhappy because they haven't taken the time to reflect upon what they have. I've seen other people struggling through sickness, loss, betrayal, and other difficult situations who still manage to focus on what is positive in their lives and feel grateful. These are the truly happy people.

Take the time, even if you are feeling frazzled, overworked, or frustrated, to ponder the things in your life that are good. Think about what you mean to those children in your class. Think about what you are offering them. Think about the fact that, for some of these children, your presence constitutes a safe harbor, perhaps the only safe harbor in their lives. Think about the professors who taught you, think about the colleagues who are helping and supporting you, think about the privilege it is to educate children, and be grateful. The attitude you bring to your school and to the children in your classroom changes the world for them and for you.

You have the power in this profession to live a fairly autonomous work life. You decide what each day will bring.

You decide whether you choose to be grateful and happy or whether you choose to join with the minority who will always find the negative. It's true that we see what we're looking for. If you are looking for joy, if you are looking for happiness, if you were looking for the best in people, that's exactly what you'll find. If you are looking for the worst in the children, in your colleagues, in the parents or the principal, that's what you will see. It's all there in the world, it's just a matter of what you choose to focus on.

GIVING BACK

A handwritten thank you note to the teacher who is always there to answer your questions and never seems impatient will mean the world to him. A note to one of your students will be forever treasured.

When I was in the second grade, many decades ago, I mustered up the courage to tell my teacher about a little sparrow that had died in our yard and how my father and I had buried it. The very next day That teacher handed me a small, sealed envelope to take home to my father. He read the note to me and I still remember what it said so many years later.

> *No wonder you have such a dear little girl. You are a father who would take the time to bury a little bird.*

I will never forget that note, and I suspect my father never forgot it either.

We have the power to bring such joy and happiness to

others by being mindful and grateful and letting them know how much their efforts, words, or kindnesses have meant to us. If you want to be truly happy in your profession, take the time each week to write a message to someone who has made an impact on you…. large or small. You will be nurturing their souls while you nurture your own, and you will become a finer person.

AND IN CONCLUSION

Winston Churchill said, "Never, never, never, give up." Great advice. I would add a few more "nevers" for new teachers.

- *Never, never, never get discouraged. Tomorrow is another day.*
- *Never, never, never underestimate your power to change lives.*

You deserve to be happy in your profession. Life is indeed very short and to spend it being upset, critical of others, whiny, sad, mopey, or petulant is a terrible waste of the gift of a life. And besides, no child deserves to come to school every day and face that kind of teacher.

For those of you who have read this book and pondered some of the ideas, I wish you success and happiness in your work, certainly, but in all aspects of your life. Invest in yourself. Care about yourself and those around you. Be happy!

REFERENCES

Bandura, A. (1997). *Self-efficacy: The reflection of control.* Freeman.

Brown, B. (2010). *The gifts of imperfection: Let go of who you think you're supposed to be and embrace who you are.* Hazelden.

Csikszentmihalyi, M. (2009). *The psychology of optimal experience.* Harper Collins.

deCharms, R. (1968). *Personal causation.* Academic Press.

Hanson, R., & Hanson, F. (2018). *Resilient: How to grow an unshakeable core of calm, strength, and happiness.* Harmony.

Huppert, F. A. (2009). Psychological well-being: Evidence regarding its causes and consequences. *Applied Psychology: Health and Well-being, 1,* 907-925.

Joshanloo, M. (2017). Mediators of the relationship between externality of happiness and subjective well-being. *Personality and Individual Differences, 11,* 147-151.

Myers, D. G., & Diener, E. (2018). The scientific pursuit of happiness. *Perspectives on Psychological Science, 13*(2), 218-225.

Palombo, M. (2003). A network that puts the net to work. *Journal of Staff Development, 24*(1), 24-28.

Yildirim, M., & Alanazi, Z. S. (2018). Gratitude and life satisfaction: Mediating role of perceived stress. *International Journal of Psychological Studies, 10*(3), 21-28.

Yildirim, M., & Belen, H. (2019). The role of resilience in the relationships between externality of happiness and subjective well-being and flourishing: A structural equation model approach. *Journal of Positive Psychology and Wellbeing, 3*(1), 62-76.

White, R. W. (1963). *Ego and reality in psychoanalytic theory.* International Universities Press.

Made in the USA
Monee, IL
21 April 2022

95152917R00125